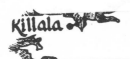

THE great tide of rebellion sweeps into the town of Ballymena, the rebels in jubilant mood, smiling and shouting, waving green branches and flags. This is the first day of liberty ...

At Shane Castle, Colonel Clavering, the British officer charged with suppressing the Rebellion, sees the United Irishmen as nothing more than the black flies of Lough Neagh, troublesome insects to be sought out and exterminated ...

Suddenly, in the long hot summer of 1798, normal life in a small town is disrupted. The crops lie untended, and, as the rebels fade into the hills, the bewildered citizens find themselves enmeshed in a shadowy world of informers and spies, where the suspicion of treachery, a careless word, can mean flogging, hazel-whipping, transportation or summary execution. Even the gentle Moravian settlement at Gracehill, which offers shelter to all creeds, finds itself under attack.

In Search of the Liberty Tree is a compelling story of those fearful days, when no quarter was given on either side, seen through the eyes of young Joshua Watson and his friend Sammy. They become, unwittingly, part of the plot to send one of the rebels into exile – in a barrel – and witness the final hunting down of the last United Irishman to hold out.

Jimmy the Post arrives at Watson's inn

Tom McCaughren

In search of the LIBERTY TREE

Illustrated by Terry Myler

ANVIL BOOKS

First published 1994 by
Anvil Books
45 Palmerston Road, Dublin 6
Paperback edition 1995

ISBN 0 947962 84 0 hardback
ISBN 0 947962 89 1 paperback

Cover: *The Battle of Ballynahinch* by Thomas Robinson
Courtesy of the Office of Public Works

Origination Computertype Ltd.
Printing Colour Books Ltd

Dedication

Some years ago, Dr Eull Dunlop,
secretary of the Mid-Antrim Historical Group,
asked me to set one of my stories in an area of the
county where a unique religious settlement had been
founded in the eighteenth century.
Subsequently I discovered that diaries kept
in the settlement record the dramatic encounters
its members had with the United Irishmen,
including the rebel leader and outlaw,
Thomas Archer. Although a work of fiction,
In Search of the Liberty Tree reflects some
of those encounters and was written in
response to Eull's request. As a result I would
like to dedicate my book to him.

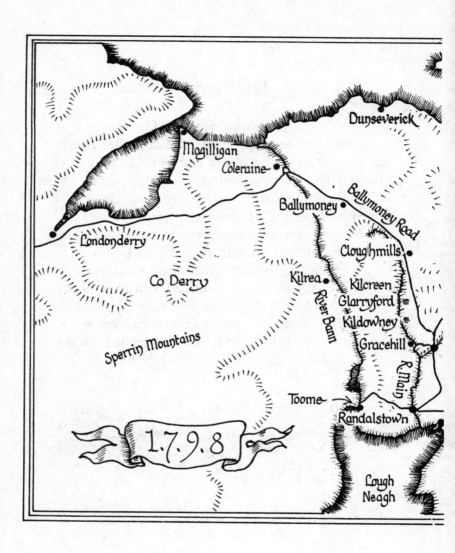

Contents

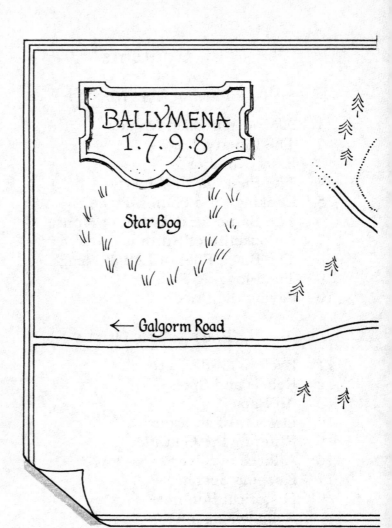

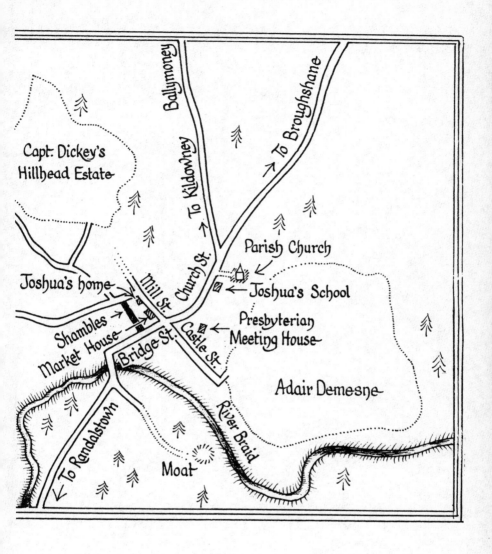

PART 1

THE MASTER

Market day at Ballymena

A Monster Called Moiley

A heat haze hung over the valley and those who were old enough to know said that it was going to be a long hot summer.

High above it all, crofters tended their sheep and pigs on the slopes of Slemish Mountain where, according to tradition, St Patrick had herded swine centuries before.

Across the valley and beyond their gaze, the calm waters of Ireland's largest lake shimmered in the heat. Those who harvested eels looked down at its everchanging images and thought of their turbulent past.

Like the crofters on the mountain the fishermen also contemplated things to come. Some said they were dreaming; others called it rebellion.

In the town that sat in the centre of the county – a fact that may have given it the name Ballymena, meaning middlemost town – it was market day.

Many had spent the morning buying and selling farm produce of one kind or another, while cottage weavers had sold webs of brown linen to bleachers who would spread it on greens and wash it with sun until it was white.

The business done, horses and donkeys stood idly on the cobbled streets outside the inns. Now and then their shoulders trembled, as blood-sucking clegs pierced their skin. They flicked their tails but the flies were out of range and could not be shifted, any more than the flat carts whose shafts hung from the heavy harness on their backs.

Other flies fed on the dung of the animals, some of which held a hind leg forward on the top of the hoof as if to ease their weight, a stance that showed they had been standing there longer than the carters would have admitted.

Here and there women in dark shawls and barefooted

children waited for their menfolk to take them home.
Oblivious to the smell of fresh dung and stale ale, they
were conscious only of their own misery.

Inside the inns men gathered in clusters in dark corners
and drank what was advertised as strong well-flavoured
Antrim whiskey. They spoke in whispers and glanced at
strangers in a way that suggested either conspiracy, or fear
of conspiracy.

In a back room at Watson's Inn, which was noted as the
place where the mail carrier called with the latest news,
young Joshua Watson was getting ready to go out and
warning his sister not to follow him.

'If you do,' he told her solemnly, 'the moiley cow will
get you – and you know what it'll do. It's a monster. It'll
eat you?'

'Joshua,' said his mother just as solemnly, 'I told you
not to be frightening Naomi with those stories. She won't
be able to sleep if you do.'

'I know,' said Joshua, 'but she'd better not follow me.
It's too dangerous.'

'I will if I want,' shouted Naomi. 'Anyway, Daddy says
a moiley's a cow with no horns. So it's not a bit dangerous.'

Joshua looked at his mother. How could they explain to
a six-year-old that in these days of rebellion the word
moiley had a much more sinister meaning.

'Don't worry,' his mother whispered, 'I'll make sure she
doesn't follow you. Now there's the money for the
camomile and a little bit extra that I owe Sister Hannah.
And be careful yourself. The country's full of United
Irishmen, not to mention beggars and thieves and good-
ness knows what else.'

He held out a small linen pouch, and when she had
dropped the coins into it he pulled it tight, tucked it inside
the waist of his breeches and tied the string to an inside
button.

'At least they won't get the money,' said Joshua, and

added with a smile, 'Unless they take my breeches as well!'

His father, who had just come in in time to hear what was being said, told him, 'You can smile, but many a man has lost the coat off his back. Remember what I told you about my father.'

Joshua nodded, 'I'd be so lucky.' He had often heard the story of how his grandfather had been accosted one night by a footpad who had forced him to exchange coats before making off into the darkness. The coat he was left with was nothing more than a smelly rag, but in one of the pockets was a gold guinea that had probably been stolen from someone else. Realizing that the footpad would soon discover his mistake, his grandfather had concealed himself among the bushes. Sure enough, the robber had come charging back a short time later, only to search in vain for his victim – and his guinea.

'Anyway,' Joshua added, 'These are my old breeches, and I'm only going to Gracehill. Sammy's going with me.'

Mr Watson nodded, and turning to his wife told her, 'There's more bread and cheese needed outside.'

He took up a tray with a jug of locally brewed ale and returned to his customers, while his wife disappeared into the recesses of the back rooms, a protesting Naomi holding on by the folds of her long black dress.

Leaving by the side door, Joshua hurried past the stables and down a narrow alley to an area of small thatched cabins called the Shambles. There, among hens that rooted around for any morsel of food they could find, and dogs that dozed in the sun, several young girls in long dirty dresses played in the dust. As soon as they were able they would play their part in the weaving of linen, winding yarn on to bobbins for use by the weaver. When that day came, their childhood would be over.

Joshua shushed a hen that was perched on a green half-door and shouted in, "Are you there, Sammy?"

From the dark interior, his friend emerged. There was a

piece of white tow on his mousy hair, evidence, if any was needed, that he had been assisting his father in the laborious job of making linen on the handloom.

'Are you ready?' Joshua asked him.

'Not just yet,' Sammy replied. 'I'll join you as soon as I can.'

'Right. I'll wait for you up at the Moat.'

Joshua went back up the alley and as he emerged into Mill Street at the front of the inn, he stopped to watch a detachment of the Antrim Militia go past.

The militiamen, he could see, were kitted out with back-packs and bed-rolls, and they marched to the beat of a single drum. Their scarlet coats seemed to glow in the sunshine, and contrasted sharply with their white collars, cuffs, and breeches. Each of them carried a musket which he had heard them call a brown bess. Bayonets and ammunition pouches hung from the ends of their white cross-belts, and he knew that when the bayonets were fitted to the end of the muskets they would be as high as their cocked hats, if not higher.

Others watched their passing too, for the word was that they were going to postings in Carlow and Wexford. Formed in each county in time of trouble to support the regular troops, the militiamen were officered by members of the Protestant gentry. However, in keeping with tradition, they served in other counties where they wouldn't have local sympathies. And so the Antrim Militia were going south, while the Monaghan Militia had come north to Antrim.

As they passed, Joshua saw that the militiamen had collected two new 'recruits' on their march through the town. Timmy Corr and Matty Meek had joined in and were striding along behind them, swinging their arms and legs in a greatly exaggerated manner to the amusement of those who had stopped to watch.

Both were beaming, and when Joshua joined them Timmy asked, 'Would I make good soldier, Jackie:'

Timmy had grown into a man, but his mind hadn't grown apace. That was why he called everybody Jackie. Matty, on the other hand, wasn't much more than four feet high, but apart from the fact that he never seemed to act his age there was nothing wrong with his mind.

'You'd both make fine soldiers,' Joshua replied, and with that assurance, they threw back their heads, smiled the smile of fools and strode on.

Joshua went with them as far as the Market House, which stood in a corner of the cross-roads at the centre of the town, and when they turned right to go down towards the bridge over the River Braid, he continued across into Castle Street.

At the top of the street he waved to Constable William Crawford, who lived in the porter's lodge at the entrance to the grounds of the Adair family, known locally as the demesne. Whatever the weather, Mr Crawford wore a tall hat and long buttoned coat which resembled a uniform. Besides manning the gate, he kept an eye on the town for Mr Adair, who was the local landlord.

'Mind how you go,' he called, but Joshua was gone. Holding on to his hat, he slid down the wooded slope until he came to the river. Pausing only to take off his shoes and stockings, he acknowledged the greetings of several women who were washing clothes in the river and waded across at a spot where the dry weather had left the water unusually low.

By the time he had climbed the great earthen mound on the far side, he was breathless and flung himself down on top. The militiamen, he could see, had crossed the bridge, leaving Timmy and Matty to find other forms of amusement in the town. Slowly but surely the soldiers marched on, their faces set firmly on the narrow road before them and he reckoned they were heading for Randalstown on the way to Belfast. He watched until their scarlet figures had faded into the distance, then turned around to wait for Sammy.

From the top of the Moat, as the mound was called, Joshua could see for miles around, the hills of Craigbilly on the right, the village of Broughshane somewhere to the left, and in between the River Braid winding its way through the valley. Dominating it all was the squat outline of Slemish Mountain. According to his schoolmaster, Mr Davison, the mountain's name was originally *Slieve Mis*, but what it meant was something of a mystery. Master Davison was a very learned man, and at a time when only a few had education and many had none, he had the distinction of being well versed in Latin and Greek. He also had a good knowledge of the Irish language, although his loyalty was to the King's English, for he was a staunch supporter of the king.

From what the master had said, Joshua had come to understand that in the not too distant past much of the countryside had been covered with oak trees. Indeed, it was still fairly well covered with trees of one kind or another, and as he shaded his eyes from the sun with his hand, he wondered if there really were thousands of United Irishmen hiding in them, waiting, as rumour had it, for the right time to rise and swamp them all. If that day came, what would they do? Where would they go?

Hearing Sammy's voice, Joshua saw his friend fording the river and answered his call with a wave. His forebodings forgotten, at least for the moment, he scrambled down to a tall ash-tree that grew on the edge of a cart track at the bottom of the mound. Nearby an old woman was prodding around with a stick. Two pigs, which might or might not have been in her care, were using their snouts to turn the ground with even greater vigour. Fearing that they might come upon his jacket and shoes if he hid them in the bushes, he climbed the tree, and when out of sight among the foliage wedged them firmly between two branches.

As soon as Sammy had got his breath back, they crossed the river by the bridge and headed out into the woodland that lay between them and the Moravian settlement at Gracehill.

At first they found the dusty road warm and pleasing to their bare feet, while their hats, which were the custom for young and old, shaded them from a sun that had shone every day since the arrival of summer. Some people, they could see, were already making their way home, either walking or sitting with their legs dangling over the sides of carts. Thinking that a cart ride might be better than walking, they pulled themselves up on to the back of one. However, mud which had been churned up by the wheels of the same carts in winter, had dried in the sun leaving the road deeply rutted and the cart was anything but comfortable. Walking on the ruts also became difficult, so after a while they abandoned the road for the woods.

'I didn't think you'd really be able to get away,' said Joshua.

'I didn't either,' Sammy told him. 'But my father needs some things from Jemmy O'Brien.'

'What sort of things?'

'Rope, and things like that.'

They walked on, and Sammy added, 'What are you getting at Gracehill, anyway?'

'Camomile.'

'Camomile? Why, what's wrong with you?'

'Nothing's wrong with me,' Joshua replied. 'My mother uses it to make tea when she hasn't any real tea.'

'Tea!' said Sammy. 'I thought it was for curing toothaches and things.'

'It does that too,' Joshua told him. 'Sister Hannah says it's a herb.'

'What's the name of the brother you go to see? The one you said is always doing the woodcarving?'

'Brother Fridlezius.'

'That's a funny name,' said Sammy. 'And another thing, why do they call themselves Moravians?'

'Because they come from Moravia,' Joshua replied.

'Where's that?'

'Brother Fridlezius says it's an ancient kingdom some-where in Europe. At least, that's where they started. Then they went to Germany, then came here.'

'Are they Protestants?' asked Sammy.

Joshua nodded. 'According to Brother Fridlezius they're the oldest Protestant Church. He says they were formed almost a century before the Reformation.'

'And why did they come here?'

Joshua smiled. 'They nearly didn't. Brother Fridlezius says they were the first Protestant Church to send out missionaries, but when their first preacher came here he got a hostile reception.'

'Who from?' asked Sammy.

'From your people.'

'You mean, the Presbyterians?'

Joshua nodded. 'Apparently Captain Adair whipped him and threatened to run him through with his sword. But he persevered, and set up a Moravian community. Later Lord O'Neill gave them the land out at Bally-kennedy, which they renamed Gracehill.'

'Is it true what they say?' asked Sammy. 'That the men and women sit on different sides of the church?'

Joshua shrugged. 'There's one door for men and one for women all right. It's the same with the avenues leading up to the graveyard. One's for men, the other for women. But whether it's just single people that are separated, or whether it applies to them all, I don't know.'

'Why didn't you ask Brother Frid . . . what's his name?'

Joshua shrugged again. 'I thought of asking him once or twice, but I didn't like to.'

Sammy lapsed into silence, and seeing that he was probably still thinking about it, Joshua wondered why he had not had the courage to ask Brother Fridlezius about the separation of the sexes. Maybe, he reflected, it was because he felt that the way they worshipped was their own business. Or perhaps it was because of the fact that their graveyard was so precious to them that they called it God's acre. That was it, he thought, it was too personal, too private, not something an outsider should be asking about.

They were thus engaged in their own thoughts when two men jumped out of the bushes, one armed with a sword, the other with a pistol. Startled, they stepped back, their hands raised in a hesitant fashion, for in their fright they didn't know what to do.

'Don't shoot, don't shoot,' shouted Sammy.

The man with the pistol told his friend to go and see if anyone else was coming. He was quite young and they could see a lot of freckles beneath his black three-cornered hat. They could also see the tip of a sword protruding from the end of his coat.

'We haven't anything worth stealing,' Joshua assured him. 'We've no money. Look.'

'Keep your hands up,' he ordered, and Joshua quickly abandoned the idea of pulling out his pockets to show they were empty.

As the other man returned, a third emerged from a thicket nearby and demanded to know what was going on. He was short in stature, strongly built and of a dark complexion, but what caught the attention of Joshua and Sammy more than anything else was the fact that under his green swallow-tailed coat, he had two pistols tucked into the belt of his breeches, while in his right hand he carried a blunderbuss He was sweating but had all the appearance of a man who would divest himself of neither his coat nor his guns, whatever the heat or the situation. 'What are you doing here?' he demanded.

Seeing the way the barrel of the blunderbuss widened out at the end like a trumpet, and realizing the damage it could do to them if it went off, they did their best to explain, which wasn't easy as they were now in a state of considerable fright.

'Gracehill,' spluttered Joshua. 'I'm going to Gracehill.'

'Ah, the brethren over at God's acre.' The man turned to Sammy. 'And what about you?'

'I . . . I'm going to see Jemmy O'Brien at the Star Bog. I have to get some things for my father.'

'Jemmy O'Brien? And what business would your father have with a layabout like him?'

'My father's a weaver. Nathaniel Johnston. We've a cabin down in the Shambles. He asked me to get some rope from Mr O'Brien.'

The man's eyes lit up and he declared, 'A weaver! Is he a Dissenter? One of ours perhaps?'

'How do you mean?' asked Sammy.

The man leaned closer. 'I mean, is he a United Irishman?'

'He is, he is,' Sammy almost shouted back, but then, seeing the way Joshua was looking at him, added, 'Well, he was. At least I think he was. I don't know.'

The man grinned. 'Then maybe we should give him a call sometime, just to make sure.' The smile was gone and he added, 'There are lots of weavers in our ranks you know, for the liberty tree is spreading. Soon the peasantry will rise up, united and strong, and when they do there'll be no rich, no poor. Everyone will be equal.' He turned to Joshua. 'And your friend here, who's he?'

In view of what had just been said, Sammy reckoned that the men might not be so well disposed to the son of someone who didn't come within the category of peasants or weavers, so he said, 'I'm Sammy Johnston. This is my brother, Joshua.'

The man's eyes lit up again. 'Joshua is it? I see you didn't bring your trumpet!' He threw back his dark head and laughed loudly at his own joke. The other two men, who were both younger, joined in the laughter, and hearing the merriment several others now emerged from the thicket.

'What's happening?' asked one of them, a tall, thin man whose height was accentuated by his long black coat and tall hat.

'This is Joshua, Doc. But he hasn't brought his trumpet.' The dark-haired man laughed loudly again and, waving his blunderbuss, declared, 'This is the only trumpet that will bring down the walls of the kingdom of George the Third.'

'Who are they and what are they doing here?' The speaker was another man who had come out of the thicket. He was young and fair-haired, and also had two pistols tucked into his belt, although he had discarded his coat in favour of his shirt-sleeves.

The man with the blunderbuss was now staring into Sammy's face, and said pointedly, "Whoever they are, Roddy, I hope they're not spying on us.'

Sammy shook his head vigorously. 'We're not spying. We were just walking along minding our own business.'

Moving closer, their inquisitor pushed Joshua's hat up with the end of the blunderbuss and, glancing at Sammy, remarked, 'You don't look like brothers.' He eyed Joshua's fair hair and fresh complexion. 'And you don't look like the son of a weaver.'

'Leave them be, Tom,' said the young man with the freckles, who seemed to have been acting as a sentry. 'I think they just came upon us by accident.'

'But they have come upon us nevertheless,' said the man with the blunderbuss.

'We won't tell anyone,' cried Joshua. 'Honest we won't.'

'Tell them what will happen if they do,' said the one called Doc.

The man with the blunderbuss grinned and told them, 'You know what happens to informers, don't you?' Before they could answer, he pressed a catch near the flintlock of his blunderbuss. A sharp-pointed bayonet that had been folded back along the brass barrel, flicked forward and came to rest within inches of their ashen faces. 'We feed them to a monster called moiley. Perhaps you've heard of her?'

When they nodded, he added, 'And you know what that means, don't you?'

'It means,' said the man with the tall hat, 'that you'll never be heard of again. For the moiley is a cow that has a huge appetite, especially for informers.'

'Will we let them go so?' The young sentry who had spoken up for them earlier was obviously anxious that they should be on their way before any blood was spilt.

The man with the blunderbuss looked at those he called Roddy and Doc. They nodded, and folding the bayonet back along the barrel of his gun he told the boys, 'All right. Off with you. But remember. One word about this, and the moiley will come looking for you.'

'Aye, in the dead of night,' said the Doc. 'When you're asleep.'

Joshua and Sammy needed no further bidding. Taking to their heels, they ran for their lives and didn't stop until they were sure they had left the men far behind.

2

The Liberty Tree

The sweeping branches of a tall beech tree moved to and fro in the slight summer breeze, dissecting the rays of the sun so that they dropped on the two boys below like ears of corn falling from a farmer's sieve.

Sammy and Joshua had flung themselves in behind the sturdy trunk and were sitting with their backs against it waiting until they got their breath back. Now and then Joshua would peep around the tree to make sure they weren't being followed and when he saw there was no one coming, let his head loll back in a gesture that indicated he was not only winded but frightened.

For a moment they watched the sun dappling their outstretched legs with changing patterns of light. They were still panting, and when they had regained enough breath to talk, Joshua said, 'That was quick thinking, telling them your father was a United Irishman.'

'So he was,' Sammy told him.

Joshua turned, a look of incredulity on his face. 'Are you serious?'

Sammy nodded. 'That was before they took up arms. He isn't any more.'

'But why?' asked Joshua. 'Why did he join them?'

'Why not?' said Sammy. 'All they were asking for was that everybody should be treated the same.'

'What do you mean the same?'

Sammy shrugged. 'I don't know. A fair share of whatever was going, I suppose. What's wrong with that?'

Joshua thought for a moment before replying, 'Nothing I suppose. But you're certain he's not in it now?'

'Of course I am. Sure I wouldn't be telling you if he was. He hasn't had anything to do with them for a long time.'

Both fell silent, each now feeling a little strange with the other.

'Anyway,' said Joshua after a while, 'I'm glad you didn't tell them who I really was.'

'I thought they'd be better disposed to us if they thought we were both weavers,' Sammy explained.

Their breathing was almost back to normal, and Sammy was beginning to worry in case he had said too much. 'What I told you about my father being in the United movement,' he added, 'you won't tell anybody, will you?'

'Why should I,' said Joshua, 'if he's not in it now.'

'Well, it's just that if anybody else heard it, they might get the wrong idea.'

'You mean the military?'

Sammy nodded. 'If they thought he was still in it they might flog him for information. Maybe burn the cabin.' When Joshua didn't reply, he added, 'They might even hang him or transport him to Van Diemen's Land.'

'Don't worry, I won't say anything,' Joshua assured him. 'But, mind you, it's not the military I'm worried about. It's the United Irishmen and what they might do.' He had closed his eyes and was thinking about some of the stories his father had read from the paper to those who gathered at the inn. Almost daily, it seemed, arms were being stolen from people in remote areas who were loyal to the Crown. Some had been murdered in their beds, others flogged. And those who were foolish enough to inform on the rebels, either to save their lives or collect a reward, would disappear without trace, 'eaten' by what was laughingly called the moiley cow.

'Do you think they meant it?' he wondered. 'I mean, what they said about the moiley coming in the middle of the night if we tell?'

'Of course they did,' Sammy replied. 'Say nothing about it or you could put us all in danger.'

Joshua looked up at the sunlight filtering through the gently swaying branches. 'What did he mean when he said the liberty tree was spreading all over the kingdom? What's the liberty tree?'

Sammy shook his head. 'I don't know ... Come on. And remember what I said. Say nothing, or we'll both be in trouble.'

They hurried on through the trees and soon they came to an area called Galgorm Parks. There they branched off towards the Star Bog, having decided they would get the things from Jemmy O'Brien first and hide them until they were coming back from Gracehill.

Jemmy O'Brien was a chandler and general jobber. He dealt in ropes and did odd jobs, although it was well known that he was lazy and that he only worked when he wanted money to buy drink. Generally speaking he kept to himself, but he was a dour man and when under the influence of alcohol, troublesome. Joshua's father had thrown him out of the inn on several occasions, and it was for this reason that Joshua now hung back among the sally bushes as Sammy went up to the cabin. Joshua could see O'Brien sitting outside, a hardy little man with a tight waist and strong arms. According to Master Davison, a chandler was someone who dealt in ropes, canvas and other supplies for ships, but there was no suggestion that Jemmy O'Brien had ever had anything to do with ships.

When Sammy staggered back with a big coil of rope around his shoulder, Joshua helped him to lug it back through the trees to the spot where they had branched off. There Joshua proposed that his friend could wait for him if he liked, but Sammy was adamant. He hid the rope under a clump of bushes and insisted that he was going to Gracehill too.

Joshua smiled. He knew well that Sammy's interest in Gracehill was the boarding-school for young ladies which had recently been opened there. Indeed, it was something that had been exercising his own mind. But now he also wanted to ask Brother Fridlezius about the men they had

The Moravian settlement at Gracehill

met in the woods.

Coming to the River Main, which eventually joined the Braid and flowed into Lough Neagh, they crossed over into the Moravian settlement. Unlike their own town, which was basically a collection of slated buildings and thatched cabins that had grown up around a cross-roads, Gracehill had been carefully laid out and was a very clean and orderly place. According to Brother Fridlezius, the founders had taken great care to map it out and, using local black stone, together with timber and slates which they had shipped across Lough Neagh from Newry, they had constructed the most modern village in the country.

The two-storey houses were built around a square that contained a fish-pond. The square in turn was hedged around with thorn and the walks shaded with rows of trees. While some of their cottages were thatched, they were of an altogether sturdier construction than the majority of cabins in the neighbourhood, and the practice of allowing animals and humans to live under the one roof was not allowed.

At the top of the square was the church, with the minister's house at one end and the warden's house at the other. On either side were the avenues lined with yew trees that led to the burial ground which they called God's acre, and once again Joshua couldn't help wondering about the Moravian custom of separating the sexes.

Whatever the rules and regulations that applied in the settlement, the brethren were known to be very progressive when it came to education. The opening of a boarding-school for young ladies had caused quite a stir in the neighbourhood, not least in the minds of young stalwarts like Joshua and Sammy.

When they arrived at the square, they dallied for a time in the hope of catching the eye of some of its attractive boarders. Several coaches belonging to members of the gentry were lined up on one side and coats-of-arms on the doors of some of them indicated that the owners were titled people. Coachmen in top hats and brightly coloured coats waited with the horses, and Joshua told Sammy that some of the girls' parents had come to visit them.

The two of them were standing on their toes looking over the hedge, to see if any of the girls had gone into the square to talk with their parents, when a voice called down asking if they were all right. Looking up, they saw that some of the brethren were still working on a turret that would give the church a clock and bell.

Feeling more than a little embarrassed, Joshua shouted back, 'I'm looking for Brother Fridlezius.'

One of the brethren pointed down behind the church, so Joshua told Sammy to wait for him and hurried round to the stone cottage at the back.

Brother Fridlezius looked after the general running of the settlement. Having come from Zeist in Holland, he had taken a wife the previous year and they now lived in the warden's house at one end of the church. The small cottage at the back was just across the yard from the stables. It was used for repairing harness and also doubled as his workshop.

When Joshua had first met Brother Fridlezius, he was surprised that a man of religion, for he seemed to be a minister, should also work as a woodcarver. It was only later that he came to understand that the settlement was self-sufficient and that all who lived there had to work. If they didn't labour on the farm, they worked as saddlers, hosiers, carpenters, tailors, shoemakers, weavers, and brushmakers, trades that were taught from an early age.

Brother Fridlezius was tall and gaunt, and like all the other brethren wore a three-quarter-length black coat and black breeches. This gave him a rather severe look, but in fact Joshua found him easy to talk to. He had been working for some time on a carving about three feet long and half as high. As it had taken shape, Joshua had seen two closely leaved branches sweeping down and out from an oval centre, and then larger leaves spreading up and out on either side.

Brother Fridlezius had explained that it was one of two carvings which he planned to put above the front doors of the church. He dislodged some shavings with his forefinger and blew the carving clean. 'Well, Joshua,' he said, 'What brings you out to the Place today?'

Joshua had come to know that all the brethren, and the sisters, called the settlement the Place. Perhaps it was a term of affection for the place in which they had decided to settle. He wasn't sure, but it seemed the most likely explanation. 'Sister Hannah,' he replied. 'I've come to see Sister Hannah. My mother wants camomile tea.'

'She's probably over in the single sisters' house.'

Watching the great care with which he carved out the leaves, Joshua asked him, 'Do you know what the liberty tree is?'

Brother Fridlezius stopped. A rare smiled flickered across his pale, bony face and he said, 'Well, whatever it is, this is not it.'

'And what is that you're doing?'

'Some might see it as representing the spread of Christianity.'

'And the liberty tree?'

Brother Fridlezius continued with his carving. 'The liberty tree represents the spread of rebellion. Anyway, who's been filling your head with things like that?

Certain in his own mind that Brother Fridlezius wouldn't break a confidence, Joshua told him about the men Sammy and he had encountered on the way.

'Short and dark you say? Sounds like Thomas Archer. He's a United Irishman all right.'

'And the others?'

'The fair-haired one they called Roddy – that must have been young McCorley from Toome over there at Lough Neagh. The other has to be the one they call Dr Linn.'

'Is he really a doctor?'

Brother Fridlezius shook his head. 'I believe he served a

short time to a surgeon and apothecary somewhere in the neighbourhood. I suppose that's where he got the name. But a little knowledge can be a dangerous thing, especially when it's about medicine.'

'What do you think they were doing there?'

'Oh, plotting rebellion, as usual.'

'And why do they call themselves United Irishmen?'

'Because, that's their aim – to see Irishmen united, be they Catholic, Protestant or Dissenter.'

'You mean, against the Crown?'

Brother Fridlezius nodded. 'That's the way it has turned out. From what I hear, young McCorley has a big following among all creeds over in the Lough Neagh area.'

'What do you mean, all creeds?'

'I mean people of different faiths.' Brother Fridlezius picked out another piece of wood-shaving with his forefinger and added, 'According to some reports they've now joined forces with the Catholic Defenders.'

'And what about Archer?'

'He's one of the leaders in this area, which as you know is mainly Presbyterian, but they seem to have supporters among all creeds around here too.'

'Has anybody left the settlement to join them?'

Brother Fridlezius hesitated. 'Just one.'

Sensing that this was something he didn't want to talk about, Joshua asked, 'Is it true Archer's from Ballymena?'

Brother Fridlezius nodded again. 'His parents live up in Castle Street, just beyond the Market House. But, of course, he's been on the run for a long time.'

'How come?' asked Joshua.

'Well, they say he started life as a shoemaker, but that wasn't exciting enough for him, so he joined the Antrim Militia. Then he deserted and joined the United Irishmen. I'm surprised they let you go.'

'Do you think they meant it when they said they'd send the moiley after us if we told anyone?'

'Well, the less you say about seeing them the better.'

'Do you think I should tell my parents?'

'Do, but be very careful. If the military get to hear the United Irishmen have been meeting in the area, you and your friend could very well get the blame.'

'How do you know so much about them?' asked Joshua.

Brother Fridlezius laid down his carving tool and took him through to the house at the other side of the church. At the end of a long table and under the watchful eye of a portrait of their founder in Ireland, John Cennick, another brother was writing in a hard-backed book. He was shorter than Brother Fridlezius and somewhat stouter, with receding grey hair brushed back from a rather round face.

'Brother Steinhauer is our bishop and keeper of our diary,' said Brother Fridlezius.

Brother Steinhauer nodded, and, as he continued to scratch with his quill, Joshua could see that even though he was a bishop he wore the same simple black clothes as the rest of the brethren.

Brother Fridlezius went over to a recess in the corner where each year's diary was kept, and taking down the one for the previous year told Joshua, 'Anything of importance that happens in the Place is recorded in the diary. If you were to read through it, you would find that Mr Archer has paid us a visit more than once.'

'What for?' asked Joshua.

'Looking for arms, what else? Muskets, pistols, swords, powder, ball . . . anything that will help them in this rebellion they seem to be planning.'

'And did they get any?'

Brother Fridlezius shook his head. 'We delivered up all our arms and ammunition to the military a year ago.'

Opening up the diary at random, he read, 'February 16, 1797. The brethren honoured the Government's proclamation that the day be appointed as a solemn day of thanksgiving for God's wonderful prevention of bloodshed and destruction in repelling the French at Bantry ... But the setback has not ceased to stir the spirit of rebellion.'

'Are you not afraid of what will happen to you, if a rebellion does break out?' asked Joshua.

'Of course we are.' He closed the book and put it back on its shelf. 'But we've been threatened before. Some years ago it was the Hearts of Steel. They wanted guns too, but what they really wanted was our land. They issued threats in the name of General Rightall, blaming us for taking the land from the previous tenants. Fortunately we were able to show them that we got it fair and square and they eventually left us alone.'

As they walked back out, Joshua asked, 'What can you do to defend yourself if you have no guns?'

Brother Fridlezius smiled. 'Our position is very simple. When it comes to rebellion, we are loyal, but neutral. When it comes to religion, our loyalty is to the Scriptures and all Christians are welcome.'

'Archer wanted to know if Sammy's father was a Dissenter,' said Joshua. 'What did he mean?'

Brother Fridlezius sat down at his bench and took up his carving again. 'He probably wanted to know if he was a Presbyterian. You see, around here the Presbyterians are very involved in the United movement.'

'Is that why they call them Dissenters?'

Brother Fridlezius shook his head. 'I take it you've heard of the Reformation?' When Joshua nodded, he went on, 'That was when the Church in England broke away from the Church of Rome and became the Protestant Church. Well, there were those who felt the only difference was that the Church in England had the King as its head instead of the Pope. They wanted a Church ruled by elected elders or presbyters, and a simpler form of worship. And because they dissented from the official form of worship, they became known as Dissenters.'

'So Sammy's father is a Dissenter then?'

'If he's a Presbyterian he is. But,' Brother Fridlezius hastened to add, 'that doesn't mean he's a United Irishman.'

Joshua was tempted to say he wasn't so sure, but thought better of it. Instead, he asked, 'So where does my Church come into it then, the Church of Ireland?'

'Well, after the Protestant Church became the official Church in England, it became the official Church here. That means it holds a special place in the scheme of things.'

Joshua thanked Brother Fridlezius, and leaving him to continue his carving hurried off to seek out Sister Hannah. At the single sisters' house they directed him to the nursery where they grew herbs of various descriptions, and there he found her in a small stone drying shed which they called the herbarium.

The sisters of the settlement were known far and wide for their linen goods, needlework and lace. They all wore white tops with white aprons over their black skirts, the only difference in dress being the ribbon with which they tied on their white linen bonnets. A blue ribbon showed that a sister was married, a white one that she was widowed. Sister Hannah wore a pink ribbon, indicating that she was single.

Joshua had always found her a most cheerful person. She had a fresh, ruddy face, and a figure that was comfortably plump, and whatever she was doing she always seemed to be happy. As she packaged the camomile for him, she inquired about his mother and wondered when the East India Company would be bringing in new supplies of 'real' tea.

Joshua smiled. It was well known in the district that the sisters were very fond of tea.

Sister Hannah gave him the camomile and some change, and then as an afterthought added, 'And here's some mint. She can use that for tea as well.'

'Do you grow that here too?' asked Joshua.

'Of course, and a lot more.' Taking him out into the nursery she stopped here and there and invited him to rub this leaf and that between his finger and thumb. In doing so, he savoured the faint suggestion of green apple from camomile, the crisp unmistakeable tang of mint, the sweet liquorish smell of fennel and many other herbs he had never even heard of.

'Hi Joshua, are you ready yet?'

Hearing Sammy's voice, Joshua thanked Sister Hannah and hurried out. Some of the girls, they could see, were strolling around the square with their mothers, all looking very elegant in their tilted hats and long dresses. On the excuse that it was too warm for walking, their fathers had adjourned to the inn. This the enterprising brethren had built and maintained (despite some serious religious scruples) for the sale of alcohol to visitors but not for themselves.

Seating themselves on a low wall, Sammy and Joshua dangled their bare feet and flirted with the girls. Now and then they were rewarded with a coy glance from a pretty face. Thus encouraged they started to do handstands and other acrobatic acts on the wall to gain further attention. More glances and giggles followed, but whatever about the girls, their mothers weren't amused.

'Be off with you, you young ragamuffins,' cried one woman, and brandishing a small parasol she chased them all the way out of the square.

Both boys knew that their behaviour was something neither Sister Hannah nor Brother Fridlezius would have approved of either, but they just laughed and waved at the girls in a show of bravado before taking to their heels.

On the way back they collected the rope and other items which Sammy had got from Jemmy O'Brien and hidden in the bushes. Otherwise they kept well clear of the place where they had run into the United Irishmen.

On arrival at the Moat, they climbed the ash tree to retrieve Joshua's coat and shoes, and seated themselves on a sturdy branch that reached out over the cart track at the edge of the mound.

'Remember,' said Sammy. 'Don't say anything about meeting those men. I don't want the moiley coming for *me* in the middle of the night.'

Joshua was still sniffing his fingers. By placing his middle finger and thumb in his nostrils and then interchanging his first finger with them in a rapid rolling movement, he could still detect a most pleasing mixture of scents from Sister Hannah's herbs.

'If you keep doing that you won't be able to help it,' warned Sammy. 'Did you hear what I said? Don't say anything about those men we met or we'll be in trouble.'

Before Joshua could answer several yeomen came galloping up the track. Passing underneath, they reined in their horses a short distance away, and surveyed the town. They looked magnificent in their red-plumed helmets and blue tunics, their sabres and short-barrelled muskets hanging by their sides.

'What do you think?' asked one. 'Are we going to have any trouble?'

The officer in charge of the group shook his head. He and his men were from Dunseverick on the North Antrim coast but had been sent to Ballymena where they were now part of the garrison. 'Most of the townspeople are loyal,' he replied. 'Wherever there's going to be trouble, it's not going to be here.'

'I wouldn't be so sure about the rest of the district,' said another.

'They can't do much without weapons,' said the officer. 'And there can't be many of those left.'

With that they spurred their horses into action and galloped away towards the bridge.

Both Sammy and Joshua knew the officer was referring to the widespread searches that had been carried out in the north the previous year, when weapons of all shapes and sizes had been seized. They climbed back down, and watched him lead his men up towards the Market House. Somehow they couldn't help wondering if he would have spoken with the same confidence had he known about their encounter with the United Irishmen.

3

Jimmy the Post

For many a night afterwards Joshua lay awake, fearing that the United Irishmen might be coming for him. When, eventually, he did get to sleep he would have nightmares about them. He would see their faces leering at him, the tall dark figure of the Doc bending over him, or Archer pushing up the brim of his hat to have a better look at his face. Sometimes in his dreams he would see Archer grinning as he released the bayonet on his blunderbuss, and hear him laughing loudly when the sharp-pointed blade flicked forward to within inches of his face. It was all so terribly real that he would sit up with a start, only to find he had been wakened by the laughter of people drinking in the back room.

On other occasions the face of a large silly-looking cow would fill his dreams. It had a big mouth and was always munching hay, and sometimes it would come closer, slobbering all over him with its huge dribbling lips. When this happened he would wipe his face with his arms and waken to find himself in a cold sweat. Thoughts of Archer and the moiley cow also haunted him during the day. He knew it was silly, but he saw himself looking at cows with great trepidation and gave them a wide berth – just in case.

Once he thought he saw Archer himself making his way through the crowds on market day, and wondered if perhaps he was paying a secret visit to his parents up in Castle Street. Then again, it was only a fleeting glimpse, and he couldn't be sure it was him. For that reason, and the continuing fear that the United Irishmen might come for him some night, he didn't say anything about it to his parents, or even to Sammy.

It was the same fear that kept him in at nights. Because

of the continuing unrest, the district, in common with many others areas, had been 'proclaimed'. This meant that it was under martial law, and a curfew was in force. Inhabitants were required to put out all fires and lights and to remain indoors between sunset and sunrise. The object was to prevent various clandestine activities, as rumours were rife that the Catholic Defenders and other factions of the United Irishmen were meeting secretly, marching and drilling by the light of the moon and making other preparations for rebellion.

As far as Joshua's family was concerned, the curfew was no great inconvenience. While the front of the inn remained in darkness, business continued as normal in the back room. Locals who were otherwise law-abiding citizens had no problem avoiding the military and slipping down the alley for a late-night drink and a chat.

Joshua also took a new interest in the visits of the mail-carrier, for he brought much more than letters. Apart from a wealth of gossip which he gathered along the way, he carried news of the turbulent events that were occurring almost daily. Jimmy the Post, as he was called, didn't come to the inn every day, and even when he was expected there was no knowing what time he would arrive. While letters had been carried on stage-coaches on the main routes for the past eight or nine years – a development that had speeded up deliveries between the main centres – villages and towns along the narrow winding side roads had still to depend on the services of 'post-boys' like Jimmy.

Whatever the weather, Jimmy wore a crushed felt hat which was cocked somewhat casually on the back of his head, a caped greatcoat, breeches, stockings and brogues. He carried the mail in a large bag which was draped over one shoulder and rested on the opposite hip under a protective forearm. His horse carried an assortment of baggage on its sagging back so that he had to walk beside it, and Joshua reckoned that they were in perfect harmony as one seemed to be as old and as lazy as the other.

Where exactly Jimmy began his journey on the route from Belfast, or where he handed over to the next mail-carrier on the way to Ballymoney, Joshua didn't know. All he knew was that when Jimmy called at the inn he was never in any hurry to leave. His excuse, if any was requir-ed, was that his horse needed a rest and its hooves needed scraping in case it had picked up any stones. This was a job that fell to Moses, the old man who looked after the stables, as there was hardly a blacksmith in the county who hadn't been arrested for making weapons for the United Irishmen.

Word of Jimmy the Post's arrival would spread quickly, and as people crowded around to hear the latest news he was plied with liberal quantities of whiskey. When event-ually he did leave, he was invariably escorted out of the town by Timmy Corr and Matty Meek, both of whom would then see themselves as mail-carriers instead of soldiers, and much superior to any of the children who tagged along behind. What time he would arrive at the next village was anybody's guess, but everyone knew the people there wouldn't be disappointed as his store of gossip would be all the richer for his visit to the inn.

Jimmy also brought a very special piece of mail for Joshua's parents. As innkeepers, they were among the very few who could afford to have the *Belfast News-Letter* delivered to them. They were also among the very few who could read, and so it was through them that news of recent momentous events was relayed to the people of the town.

While Jimmy was still there, Joshua's father would read out the main points of the news, news which would be greeted with cheers or silence, depending on whether it was good or bad. And, whether it was good or bad, Jimmy would confirm the truth of it with a vigorous nod of his head, as if the job of carrying mail had somehow made him the fountain of all knowledge. Later, when he had gone,

Joshua's parents would take a break and pore over the paper in the privacy of their own quarters, an experience that was shared with no member of the public, except perhaps Master Davison, who was able to fill in any gaps that existed in their knowledge of politics or international affairs. Later still, when the curfew was on, those who couldn't read and wished to hear more would slip in by the side door for a drinking session that usually involved a more extensive reading than had been given at the bar.

It was in this way that people kept themselves informed of what was happening in the wars with France, and of reports that the French might be preparing for another invasion in support of the United Irishmen. Earlier in the year they had learned that the leaders of the conspiracy had been arrested in Dublin, that various outrages had been severely punished and that the military were taking steps to disarm the south in the same way they had already done in the north.

They also heard that the paper contained declarations of loyalty from those who had recently assumed the name of Orangemen and from various corps of yeomanry. The Orangemen in turn welcomed a declaration of loyalty from the Catholic inhabitants of several parishes, and assured their Catholic neighbours that they intended them no harm.

Nevertheless the turmoil continued north and south and when, at the end of the day, his father would finally lay the paper aside, Joshua would scan it himself to see if there was any news of the arrest of Thomas Archer.

He read of people being charged with high treason for 'compassing and imagining the death of the king' and 'adhering to the persons exercising the powers of Government in France in case they should invade or cause to be invaded this Kingdom of Ireland ... ' Others were being charged with administering the oath to new members of the United Irishmen, an offence punishable by death. Suspected persons, he read, were also being whipped to

induce them to make confessions of guilt and name their
accomplices, and Antrim, he saw, wasn't the only place
where blacksmiths were being arrested for making weapons.

The paper reported how one blacksmith was carried
through the streets of Dublin on horseback, his bellows
borne before him, and his person hung over with pikes
which had been found in his forge. But of Archer there
was no word. Or of the one they called Dr Linn, or of
Roddy McCorley or of any of the other United Irishmen
Sammy and he had met in the woods.

Because Sammy helped his father with the weaving, he
only went to school occasionally, and then only at the
insistence of Joshua's father who felt he had a responsibility to see that his tenants got some tuition in the three
Rs. Even when he did go, it was to a school at the Presbyterian meeting-house up the lane behind Church Street,
not the one Joshua went to. As a result it was exactly a
week after they had met the rebels before they got together
again.

'What's a pike anyway?' asked Joshua.

Sammy and he were helping Moses to clean out the
stables. They would much rather have been out playing as
there had been no break in the sunny weather, but Joshua
had been told to help Moses.

'I'm not sure,' Sammy replied. 'I think it's like a lance –
you know, like the ones the cavalry have their flags on.'

Joshua was puzzled. 'But lances are very long. I was
reading in the paper that a blacksmith was paraded
through Dublin with pikes he had made hanging around
his neck.'

Moses, who looked after the beer barrels as well as the
stables, always wore a dirty old apron and walked bent
over as if he had spent a lifetime carrying barrels or shoe-
ing horses. He smiled when he heard this, and wiping the
ends of his drooping grey moustache with the back of his
hand, told them, 'A pike is like the blade of a spear, with

an axe or sharp hook on the base of it. It's hammered out in a forge, just like a horseshoe, and that's the bit that would have been hung around the neck of the blacksmith in Dublin. They say they're being turned out by the thousand in forges all over the country. It's only when they've been fitted with long wooden shafts that they're like lances.'

'Is there really going to be a rebellion then?' asked Joshua.

'It's looking powerful like it,' said the old man. 'They say they're drilling in broad daylight now in some districts. And some are even cutting their hair short.'

'Why are they doing that?' asked Sammy.

'It's what the revolutionaries did in France. Instead of wearing their hair down to their shoulders like we do, they're cropping it short. That's why people are calling them croppies. They don't seem to care now whether they're recognized or not.'

Joshua had heard the name, but until now he hadn't understood what it meant. Why, he wondered to himself, had Archer and his friends not cropped their hair?

'What's going to happen?' he asked. 'I mean, if the rebellion breaks out.'

Moses cleaned his hands on his apron and assured him, 'You'll be all right. Your parents will tell you what to do.' He straightened himself up again and, looking at Sammy's pale face, said, 'Anyway, it's too nice a day to be in here talking like this – off you go and enjoy yourselves.'

Joshua's face lit up. He could see Moses was thinking that Sammy spent a long time in the gloom of his cottage helping with the weaving and could do with a bit of colour in his cheeks. 'Are you sure?' he asked.

However, Moses was bent over again, as he went about his work, and just waved them away. They thanked him and hurried up the alley into the bright sunshine of Mill Street. It was late afternoon and the voices in the inn had become appreciably louder as drink loosened tongues that had been tied up with the worries of the week.

Thankful that he hadn't been asked to help in the inn, Joshua slipped past the open door and they headed towards the Market House.

Timmy Corr was sitting on the step of the Market House, his long listless face tilted up towards the sun. Seeing them approach he jumped to his feet, for despite the slowness of his brain he sensed a certain purpose in their step. 'Hi Jackie, can we come with you?' he asked.

The small round figure of Matty Meek suddenly appeared beside him. 'Aye, can we come with you?' he mimicked. 'Are you going down to the river?'

'We're just going for a message,' Joshua told them, and wheeled left up Church Street.

Joshua and Sammy had a great affection for the two and enjoyed their antics as much as anyone else, but they also knew they could be a dreadful nuisance.

At the top of the street they cut in past the church and made their way through the graveyard. There they helped each other up over the wall and dropped down into the tranquility of the demesne.

A few steps and they were in the woods. The rooks had not yet returned from the cornfields and in the tall oak trees above pigeons cooed softly. Like the two who walked below, the pigeons were content in each other's company and the knowledge that they had the woods more or less to themselves.

'Did you ever wonder,' said Sammy, 'why they call this place "the demesne"? I mean, it's a funny word, isn't it?'

'I asked Master Davison about it once,' said Joshua. 'He says it's because the Adairs own a lot of the land around here, and this is their own private domain. It's spelt "demesne", but he says it means the same.' He smiled. 'Can you imagine coming in here with Matty and Timmy? They'd have Constable Crawford on to us like a flash.'

Sammy took off his hat, and bending his head ruffled his tousled hair with his fingers to get the dust of the loom out of it. 'We could have gone up Castle Street,' he said.

'I didn't want them following us,' Joshua explained. He was silent for a moment. 'Anyway, Archer's parents live up there. I was afraid we might run into him.'

'Sure he wouldn't dare come home,' said Sammy. 'He's a wanted man. The militia would shoot him on sight. And if the yeomen got him, they'd hang him from the nearest tree.'

Joshua nodded. 'I know. But still, I thought I saw him the other day.'

Sammy looked at him in surprise. 'You mean he was here, in the town?'

'Well, I can't be sure,' said Joshua, 'but I thought it was him.'

'Had he cut his hair short, like Moses said?'

'No, it was the same length as it was the day we met him on the way to Gracehill – down to his shoulders.'

'I'd say the last thing he wants to do is draw attention to himself,' said Sammy. 'Did you tell your mother and father you saw him again?'

Joshua shook his head.

'Why not?' asked Sammy.

'I could hardly sleep after what he said the day he stopped us,' Joshua confessed. 'About the moiley coming to get us. I had nightmares and everything. Did you not?'

'By the time I get to bed at night I'm too tired to have nightmares.'

'By the time I get finished helping in the inn some nights I can be tired too,' said Joshua. 'But I still couldn't help thinking about him and what he said he would do to us if we told anybody. What did your father say when you told him?'

Sammy shrugged. 'He said it could have been anybody.'

'How could it have been anybody?' asked Joshua. 'You saw the weapons they had, and you heard what they said about the United Irishmen. Brother Fridlezius knew exactly who he was. He knew all of them.'

Sammy took off his hat again. 'Well, my father says we're not to worry about them. He says they're too busy rebelling or whatever they're doing to be bothered about us.' He smiled and giving Joshua a dig with his elbow ran off through the trees shouting, 'Come on, I'll race you.'

Not to be outdone, Joshua chased after him, and by the time they emerged from the trees at the far side, they were neck and neck. Panting for breath, they paused for a moment to make sure there was no one around. Then, taking up the race again, they ran on down the slope to the meadows where the River Braid wound its way slowly from Broughshane.

Arriving at the river they threw themselves down, and, lying on their backs, laughed heartily at their own frivolity. When their laughter had subsided and they had got their breath back, they turned and lay looking into the river. They could feel the heat of the sun on their backs, and when they trailed a finger in the water they found it cool to their touch.

Spotting a red-breasted minnow, Sammy whispered, 'Look, spricks.'

They immediately began digging with their fingers for small worms. These they squeezed on to the points of rushes and dangled in the water as bait. In this way they landed several of the small fish, but as they had no container with them they had to throw them back again.

'Come on,' said Joshua, discarding his rush and taking off his shoes. 'Let's have a swim before we go back.'

There was another race, this time to see who could get his clothes off first, and in what seemed no time at all they were splashing about in the river, all thoughts of outlaws and rebels forgotten.

The king's health had not been good. It was reported that he suffered periodic bouts of madness, and at one stage there had even been talk that he might abdicate. However,

Toasting the king's health

he had recovered, and after war had broken out with revolutionary France in 1793 he was seen as a symbol of the
old English order of things for which the country was said
to be fighting.

In their own small way, Joshua's mother and father also
saw him as a symbol of order at a time when it seemed
that many in Ireland were bent on following France's lead
and plunging the country into rebellion. Consequently,
when they toasted the king's health on the evening of May
24th, with a cup of tea and a glass of brandy, it was
coupled with the wish that long might he reign.

Mrs Watson always kept a little bit of what she called
'real' tea for such an occasion, as it was expensive and
often in short supply. It also pleased her to see her husband taking down his long-stemmed clay pipe and enjoying a few puffs. Such moments were rare for a family that
ran a busy inn, and later, when Master Davison called,
Joshua listened quietly as they reflected on the state of the
king's health and, inevitably, the state of the nation.

'What I don't understand,' said Joshua, 'is how all this
trouble started.'

His father smiled. 'I often wonder myself.'

'I think it all started with the American revolution,' said
Master Davison. 'I remember, before you were born, the
colonists started agitating against trade restrictions and
taxes imposed by the Parliament in London. Then they
began to fight for independence.'

'What's that got to do with it?' asked Joshua.

'Well,' said the master, 'a lot of the American colonists
are descended from Ulster Presbyterians, and their actions
were watched with great interest.'

'Then the Volunteers were formed here,' said his father,
taking up the story. 'They were armed and trained in case
of a French invasion – for the French were supporting the
Americans, you see. But the Volunteers started agitating
too.'

'Like the Americans,' explained the master, 'they wanted better trading arrangements. They also wanted greater independence for the Parliament in Dublin, and they did win important concessions.'

'Eventually they were disbanded,' said his father, 'and replaced by the militia and the yeomen.'

'But then the French Revolution came on top of all these things,' the master went on. 'Their ideas of liberty and equality spread, and you had the formation of the Society of United Irishmen.'

'I think that's where it all started,' said Mrs Watson, who had been sipping her tea and listening carefully to what was being said. 'With the United movement.'

Joshua, who had also been listening carefully, was thinking of the United Irishmen he had met in the woods. From the window of his room upstairs he often looked out across the countryside towards Gracehill. It was a lovely view, and the woods always seemed so peaceful, especially towards evening. What a pity, he thought, that all this trouble should come along and spoil it.

'In a way,' the master told Mrs Watson, 'you're probably right. Much of it did start with the United movement. But I remember a time when I thought their ideas were very worthy indeed.'

Surprised, Joshua pulled his stool closer to hear what the master had to say.

'I remember,' the master continued, 'reading a pamphlet by a young Protestant barrister in Dublin by the name of Wolfe Tone. He didn't sign it at the time, mind you, but it soon became common knowledge that he was the author of it. He argued strongly for Catholic emancipation, but what really struck me was his argument about Catholic education, or rather the lack of it.'

On previous occasions, when Joshua had asked what Catholic emancipation meant, he had been told it was about equal rights, although what these rights were he wasn't quite clear, apart from the fact that they related to Parliament and the running of the country.

'At that time,' the master continued, 'Tone was pro-
fessing his loyalty to the king as King of Ireland. Then he
became a leading light in the Society of United Irishmen.
At first, I suppose, it wasn't much more than a debating
society, and I must confess the notion of people of all
creeds coming together for the good of all was one that
appealed to me. But after a while separation from England
became the objective, and of course, that was something I
couldn't accept.'

'And now we're threatened with rebellion,' said Mrs
Watson.

'Well, if it does break out,' her husband assured her, 'we
have the militia to protect us.'

'I wouldn't want to rely on them too much,' said the
master. 'I think their discipline leaves a lot to be desired.
No, if there's a rebellion, it's the yeomen who'll stand by
us. They're local and they're loyal. Their officers are all
landed people and they get their commissions direct from
the Crown.'

Mr Watson filled up the glasses, and, as the master
savoured the contents of his, Joshua detected a twinkle in
his eye.

'You know, of course,' said the master, addressing his
remarks to Mrs Watson, 'the King's birthday isn't until the
fourth of June?'

Mrs Watson sat up straight and asserted, 'If King
George was born on May 24th, he was born on May 24th,
and nobody can change that, not even the Government.'

Joshua smiled. He had often heard the master teasing
his mother about this before.

'The fact is,' continued the master, for Joshua's benefit
as much as his mother's, 'eleven days were dropped from
the calendar in 1752, so his birthday is now on the
fourth.'

'Why did they do that?' asked Joshua.

The master sipped his glass and made himself more
comfortable. 'It was necessary to bring the year back into

line with the seasons. You see, a small inaccuracy had built up over the centuries, and a new-style calendar had to be introduced to correct it. This was done by dropping eleven days. I've explained it all to your mother before, but she just won't listen.'

Mrs Watson sipped her tea and looked into the fire. Perhaps she understood. Perhaps, like Joshua, she didn't. In any case, they all knew that like her mother before her she would continue to celebrate the king's birthday on May 24th.

What none of them knew was that in the year that had now arrived, 1798, other momentous events were occurring on the same date, events that would change the course of Irish history for many generations to come.

4

The First Day of Liberty

It wasn't until May 26th, two days after the Watsons had celebrated the king's birthday, that news reached the town that the long-rumoured rebellion had broken out. It was late evening when Jimmy the Post arrived, having stopped more often and much longer than he should have, an indication in itself that he carried important news. Before he had even handed over the *News-Letter*, he announced that the rising had begun and that the capital was under martial law.

'It's true,' he declared, putting the paper down on the counter. 'The mail-coach was seized not far from Dublin. The whole place is up in arms.'

As customers crowded round, Joshua's father opened the paper and spread it out before him. His wife appeared at his side and as they scanned the latest despatches they could see the rebellion had broken out on May 23rd, the eve of the very day they had toasted the king.

'It is true,' said Mr Watson. 'Listen to this: "We stop the press to state that an express has just arrived, stating that martial law has been proclaimed in Dublin."'

'What else does it say?' shouted a man from the back.

'Aye, read it out to us,' urged another.

Mr Watson took up the paper and held it closer to his eyes. 'Here's a despatch dated Thursday, May 24th. It says: "In consequence of some information of an alarming nature received by the Government, the drum beat to arms about 12 o'clock last night, and the several corps of yeomanry in this city repaired to their alarm posts. Canon were placed in the avenues leading to the castle – the military preparations wore the most awful appearance – and a considerable degree of consternation prevailed throughout the night."'

He looked up. More people were crowding in, and seeing that they were anxious to hear more, he went on: ' "This morning led us further into the cause. A large body of insurgents had assembled between Crumlin and Tallaght, in the neighbourhood of Saggart, all armed and most of them mounted." '

'Where was this?' asked a late-comer.

'Dublin,' someone told him impatiently. 'Go on.'

Mr Watson continued: ' "They were opposed by the yeomanry in that quarter, who fired on them, but without effect, and were obliged to retreat. An express having been sent in the interim, a reinforcement of cavalry – the 5th Dragoons – arrived, between whom and the insurgents a conflict ensued in which three of the latter were killed and about thirty taken prisoners ... The insurgents were armed with pistols, swords, blunderbusses and pikes." '

'What else does it say?' another man put in.

Mr Watson read out another report: ' "On the 23rd at Clondalkin, about four miles from Dublin, on the Naas Road, a party of the 5th Dragoons and yeomen cavalry fell in with four hundred of the rebels, whom they dispersed, killed many, and brought in nine who will be brought to a court martial this evening. Three others were hanged this morning in Berwick Street, being condemned by court martial." '

'And listen to this: "Near Kilcullen there has been a very serious action. An officer of the 5th Dragoons and several men were killed and wounded by insurgents, who were at last routed and above two hundred of them killed. At Naas there was another very ferocious action, in which as many more of the insurgents were killed, without any loss on the part of the military. A great number of arms of every description are brought to the capital hourly, and there is no doubt that this rebellion will be crushed in a very few days." '

'What does it say about the mail-coach?'

'Let me see. Aye, here it is. It says information has been

received at this office – that's the General Post Office – that the mail-coach which was despatched with the mail for the north last night was stopped by a numerous band-itti near Santry, who set fire to and consumed the coach and entire mail.'

'What's banditti?' someone asked.

'Bandits,' Mr. Watson told him. 'Outlaws, probably United Irishmen. The southern coach was attacked too – at Lucan.'

As his father continued to read bits and pieces, Joshua nipped out through the side door and raced down through the stable yard to tell Sammy the news. It was just coming on to dusk, and as he emerged out into the Shambles he saw two men coming out of Sammy's cottage. He pulled up short, hardly able to believe his eyes. For a brief moment the two were framed in the dim light of the door-way; one was the short stout figure of Thomas Archer, the other the tall thin figure of Dr Linn. Sammy's father bade them goodnight, the door closed and the two slipped away into the night.

Master Davison closed his tattered copy of *Robinson Crusoe* from which he had been reading to his pupils. Usually, he knew, they looked forward to hearing the story and he was treating them to another reading in an effort to take their minds off the terrible events that now hung over the town like a dark cloud.

Daniel Defoe's story of the sailor who was shipwrecked on a tropical island had caught the public imagination when it was published and now, almost eighty years later, it still appealed to young people like Joshua and his friends in a way that no other book had done.

Today, however, even this fascinating story could not hold their attention, and, realizing that their minds were on other things, Master Davison put the book down. An imposing figure in his black frock coat, waistcoat and breeches, he considered for a moment how he might reassure them. Then, tugging with both hands at his swallow-tailed coat where it was cut square at the waist, he shrugged so that it sat more comfortably on his broad shoulders, and attempted to address some of the fears which he could see were clearly written on their young faces.

Like Joshua, the pupils of his one-roomed school in Church Street were the sons of people who were relatively well off, Protestants with land or some form of business who supported the Crown, and, now that the rebellion had begun, they feared for what the future might hold.

'I know,' he began, 'that you are all apprehensive of what may happen now that the flame of rebellion has been lit in the capital, or should I say its environs. However, it is by no means certain that the flame has taken hold, or that it will spread. By all accounts the north has not followed suit and my hope is that it won't. This may be due to the fact that General Lake moved to disarm the north last year, and the United Irishmen may not have the weapons to follow the example of their southern brethren . . .'

As Master Davison continued to analyse the situation, his words were of some comfort to his class. But when he went on to say that, in any event, certain arrangement had been made so they had nothing to worry about, Joshua knew differently. For during those meetings in the back room, when the inn had been cleared and the side door closed, he had overheard the master and his friends talking about other things.

They had spoken of how, during the French Revolution only a few years before, thousands of the king's supporters – and indeed many who weren't – had been dragged off to the guillotine by the peasant mob and beheaded in public.

'It's my information,' one of them had whispered, thinking Joshua wouldn't hear him, 'that a guillotine has already been built here.'

'Where?' asked another.

'Out near Kilrea,' was the reply.

Shocked at the news, the others had leaned forward to hear more.

'It's true,' the man had assured them. 'I'm told it's about nine feet high and has a heavy blade which is extremely sharp. The word is they've tried it out on cats and dogs. And they've drawn up a black list, so you can guess whose heads will roll if the United Irishmen rise here.'

Later, Joshua's father had sought to reassure him, and warned him not to say anything about the guillotine to his mother or to Naomi, even in jest. But the thought of being led to the guillotine came to haunt him in the same way as the thought of the moiley cow. Then, to cap it all he had seen the two rebel leaders leaving Sammy's cottage.

That had thrown his mind into such turmoil that he couldn't think straight. The side door had been closed when he returned, but he didn't want to knock. He didn't want to talk to anyone. He couldn't. So he climbed up over the beer casks that were stacked against the wall in the stable yard, and made his way across the roofs of the outhouses to his bedroom. How long he lay thinking of what had happened, he didn't know. All he could think of was the two figures framed in the doorway of the cottage and Mr Johnston bidding them goodnight. He seemed to be seeing them off in a way that suggested he knew them, and they couldn't have been there without Sammy being aware of it. After all, the cottage had only two small rooms – the kitchen and the room where they had the loom.

Now, as he thought back on it again, Joshua could still hear Master Davison's voice reassuring the class, but he was unaware of what he was saying. Things began to come into his mind, like the day they had met the rebels in the woods. What was it Archer had asked when he had heard Sammy's father was a weaver? 'Is he a Dissenter, a United Irishman perhaps?' 'He is,' Sammy had told him. Then he had changed his story. He had said his father was no longer a member, not since they had taken up arms. Why then was he consorting with Archer and Dr Linn?

Then there was Sammy's reaction when he had told him he thought he had seen Archer in town. He didn't seem to be very surprised. And he seemed to be trying to say it might not have been Archer at all that they had met in the woods. What was it Sammy's father had said? 'It could have been anybody.' Could it be that his father was still a United Irishman? Was that why he was no longer afraid?

Joshua hadn't said anything to his own father about what he had seen at the cottage as he wasn't sure what was going on and he didn't want to see Sammy's family being evicted. Nor could he bring himself to call on Sammy again. So he sought out his other friends and played with them. Somehow everything seemed to be closing in on him. He had visions of a huge tree spreading slowly over the countryside, its branches like the arms of an octopus, enveloping houses, people, livestock, everything it found in its path.

'What's the liberty tree?' he asked suddenly.

Master Davison stopped what he was saying, and the other pupils looked around.

Seeing the worried look on Joshua's face, Master Davison didn't reprimand him for the interruption as he might otherwise have done. Instead, he told him, 'During the French Revolution, trees were planted in towns and villages by way of celebration. These became known as trees of liberty. Now, by all accounts, that custom has been adopted by the United Irishmen. So also, I'm sorry to say, have the revolutionary doctrines of the French.' The master fixed him with a stern eye. 'Why, have you seen something of this nature?'

Joshua shook his head. 'No, Sir, it was just something I heard.'

Being a close friend of the Watsons, Master Davison was aware of Joshua's encounter with the United Irishmen in the woods, but not wishing to break a confidence or add to the fear of his other pupils, he didn't pursue the matter.

'All right then,' he said. 'Now, as I was saying, I've had meetings with your parents and they've made plans to ensure your safety – should trouble break out.' He tugged down the waist of his coat again, indicating more a discomfort of mind than of body, and added, 'I think it's time they told you what those plans are. So, off you go now. And remember, keep yourselves to yourselves and don't discuss these things with anyone else.'

Never was a classroom cleared with such a rush. Squeezing through the doorway the boys split up, shouting their goodbyes as they ran for home.

The plan, so far as Joshua was concerned, was simple. At the first sign of trouble in the town he was to take his sister, Naomi, and go with Moses to their Uncle Matthew's house in the townland of Kildowney, about eight miles north on the road to Ballymoney.

'You should be safe there,' his mother told him.

'And what about you?' he asked.

'Don't worry about us,' his father assured him. 'We'll be all right.'

'And what if Naomi doesn't want to go?' asked Joshua.

'We'll just tell her Moses is taking the two of you out for a run on the horse and cart.' She forced a smile. 'She likes that, so she should be all right.

'In the meantime,' said his father, 'act normally and, as Master Davison says, don't let on to anybody what we're planning to do – not even your friend Sammy.'

Joshua felt like saying Sammy was the last person he would tell, but he just asked, 'Does that mean I still have to go to school?'

'Of course it does,' said his mother. 'Didn't you hear what your father said? We just don't know who's with the United Irishmen and who's not. There are spies everywhere, so just try to act normally.'

Joshua hated going to school, especially as some of his friends didn't go, but his parents told him that those who did go were lucky to have the opportunity and Master

Davison made sure they made the most of it. Now, it seemed, even rebellion was no reason to be absent.

In the days that followed, the arrival of Jimmy the Post at the inn was awaited as never before. He brought news that the rebellion had spread southwards, engulfing towns and villages in Kildare, Wicklow, Carlow and Wexford. There were frightening reports of massacres on all sides and harrowing tales of death and destruction as the opposing forces claimed victories and defeats.

All the while the north held its breath. Some said the northern rebels were waiting for the French; others said they had been infiltrated by Government spies and that their plans had been nipped in the bud. Whatever the reason, they didn't rise and, after almost two weeks of relative calm, many believed the moment of danger had passed.

Unknown to them, thirty-five rebel leaders had already met at a place called the Sheepree on Ballyboley Hill, east of Ballymena, and decided on a date for the rebellion. In a despatch to his commanders, the United leader, Henry Joy McCracken declared, 'Army of Ulster. Tomorrow we march for Antrim ... ' Like Joshua's mother, he was writing his own calendar, and dated his message with the words, 'First year of Liberty, 6th June, 1798.'

The good weather had continued without a break, and as Joshua made his way to school he could see the sun glinting on the buttons and weapons of a troop of yeomen cavalry who were forming up outside their quarters in Castle Street, a short distance beyond the Market House.

Before turning up Church Street, he stopped to watch them. They were lining up their horses to form an escort for the coaches and carriages of some of the local gentry, and while Joshua knew he was cutting it fine he decided it was worth risking Master Davison's wrath to dally for a moment.

In fact, he wasn't the only one, for the yeomen pre-

The Dunseverick Yeoman Cavalry form an escort

sented a colourful spectacle as they trotted towards the
Market House and wheeled left into Bridge Street.

As they turned the corner, he counted sixteen of them.
Their dark blue tunics had rows and rows of buttons and
braid and their white cross-belts an oval badge of gleaming
brass. Their breeches were white and bright and tucked
into tight black riding boots which had silvery spurs. For
all that, it was their dark round helmets that impressed
him most. These had a crest of fur that swept back from
the peak like a horse's tail and were topped by a feathery
plume which was brilliant red with a tinge of white.

The carbines and sabres that hung at their sides rattled
with the movement of their horses, and the swallow-tailed
flag which fluttered from a lance in the hand of one of the
leading riders proclaimed that they were going about the
business of the king. Royal blue, the flag was fringed with
silver and had two silver tassels. In the corners, on a
background of red, were the emblems of the Crown – the
white horse of the House of Hanover in Germany from
which the king was descended, and the letters GR, the
monogram of the reigning monarch, embossed in gold.
Emblazoned in the centre was the name of their corps,
Dunseverick Yeomen Cavalry, together with scrolls in
Latin which proclaimed their faith in God and King.

It was a display that was matched only by the splendour
of the carriages and of those who sat in them. One
bystander said they were magistrates – gentry and clergy-
men – who were going to Antrim town to discuss the
disturbed state of the county with the governor, Lord
O'Neill. The yeomen, Joshua knew, were officered by such
people and, like the militia, had been formed to help the
regular regiments. Some magistrates had been murdered,
even before the trouble had broken out in the south, and
he wasn't surprised to see such a heavy escort. Five or six
yeomen had come out to see them off, and he reckoned
they had been left to maintain a presence in the town.

Wrenching his eyes away from them, Joshua hurried up

Church Street. He arrived at school breathless but in time, and when he had taken his seat saw that the master had already written the date on the blackboard. It was Thursday, June 7th.

In the Presbyterian school in the village of Broughshane, four miles away, the master dismissed his class at noon and unknown to his pupils made his way to a pre-arranged meeting place. There he changed his frock coat for a green uniform and took command of a company of United Irishmen.

The first sign of the impending rebellion came as the villagers sat down to their mid-day meal. They heard the beat of a drum on the street outside, and when the children rushed out to inquire what was happening, the drummer merely replied, 'You'll know soon enough.'

A short time later word arrived that armed men were marching down from the hills, and, before long, numerous pikes and guns were seen glittering in the sun as the rebels entered the village. Some were blowing coiled brass instruments which they called French horns, those who had uniforms wore green cockades in their hats, others sprigs of green, and, in imitation of this, children ran alongside waving branches which they had plucked from the bushes. The rebels paraded for a short time in the village and then, forming up in ranks, marched off towards Ballymena.

When word arrived that the rebels were approaching the town, Master Davison immediately dismissed his class, but, unlike the schoolmaster in Broughshane, endeavoured to rally some of the townspeople in some form of defence.

Alarmed by the news, Joshua ran home as fast as he could. In their own quarters at the back he found that his mother had already dressed Naomi in old clothes and laid out various cast-offs for himself. 'If this is a peasant revolt,' she said, 'you'd better look like one.'

Joshua nodded and proceeded to put them on, but

Naomi was complaining, 'I don't like these clothes. They're old and they're smelly.'

Her mother hunkered down beside her and holding her firmly by the arms told her, 'Now, Naomi, I want you to listen to me. Moses is taking you and Joshua to visit Uncle Matthew. You'd like that, wouldn't you?' She nodded. 'Well then, these clothes are just for the journey. The roads are dusty and dirty and you can't be wearing your good ones. You can put them on when you arrive.'

Whether this satisfied Naomi or not suddenly became unimportant. Her mother whisked her out of the side door where Moses was waiting with the horse and cart. Her father hurried out after them and threw an old bag of things up beside her, saying to Joshua, 'Take care of her now. And remember, she's only six.'

'I will,' Joshua assured them. 'And what about you?'

'We'll find a safe place,' his father replied. 'Now go. There's no time to lose.'

There was no time for further farewells either. Joshua pulled himself up on to the cart and put his arm around Naomi. Moses flicked the back of the horse with the reins, and with a click of his tongue ordered it to giddy-up. Spurred to action, it jerked forward, drawing them out of the entry and into the brightness of the street. There some people were running hither and thither, others were standing in groups talking, while some were looking out over their half-doors, wondering what was going to happen.

Outside the Market House, Master Davison was talking and gesticulating as he tried to get several yeomen and a small group of locals to agree on what to do.

Turning left up Church Street, Moses urged the horse on as fast as it would go and didn't stop until they reached a fork in the road at the top of the town. The road to the right led to Broughshane, and they were relieved to see there was no sign of the rebels. Taking the road to the left they galloped on towards Kildowney. After a few miles, however, they spotted a column of men marching towards them. Even at a distance they could see they didn't have the scarlet coats of the military. Moses immediately turned the cart and headed back to the junction. Knowing that they couldn't go back into the town, he turned up the other road, which was still clear, and waited at a safe distance for the rebels to pass. It was only then that they saw the rebels coming from Broughshane and knew they were trapped.

Fortunately, the rebels were in a festive mood. They were smiling, shouting and blowing all sorts of horns. The first day of liberty had come, they announced. They were jubilant, they were joyful, and they insisted that Moses should join them. 'Liberty, equality, fraternity,' they were chanting. The horse was now facing back towards town, and several pulled themselves up on to the cart. Dangling their legs over the sides, they raised their pikes and pitchforks in the air with shouts of 'Vive la France'.

Joshua drew Naomi closer to him and, as they moved off, he realized to his horror that they were being swept back into town on a great tide of rebellion.

5

Looking for a Hiding-Place

The flat cart was made in such a way that its solid wooden wheels were tucked well underneath, between the shafts. And while it wasn't very big, this meant that people were able to sit all along the sides without fear of getting their legs entangled in the wheels.

When there were no more spaces left, several rebels jumped up into the centre of the cart beside Joshua and Naomi. Those who didn't wear hats had a strange, cropped look about them, their hair having been cut short in the way Moses had described. Fearing they might see he wasn't one of them, Joshua pushed his hat down on the back of his head to cover his own shoulder-length hair, and put his arm further around Naomi. However, they were all in good spirits, and even though one waved a musket in the air and proclaimed that the cart had been commandeered in the name of the revolution it was done in a jovial fashion.

When the man hunkered down beside them, Joshua could see two white belts hung from his shoulders, and where they crossed on his chest there was an oval-shaped badge with an inscription that indicated it was from a uniform of the old Volunteers of Ballygarvey, a townland not far distant. The badge was directly opposite Joshua's face and he could see it also bore the words 'Liberty – Property'. Now, as he looked back, he could see more of the rebels had muskets and he reckoned a good many had kept them when the Volunteers had been disbanded.

Naomi was too young to understand what was happening, but old enough to sense danger in the general commotion, in spite of the smiling faces beside her. Turning to her brother, she caught hold of his coat and, looking up into his face, whispered, 'What's going on, Joshua?'

Joshua pulled her closer, and forcing himself to smile tried to reassure her. 'It's all right,' he told her. 'It's just a parade. Look! Look at all the flags.'

It was only then that Joshua took greater notice of the flags himself. Some were simply pieces of green cloth attached to pike shafts, others had a yellow harp without a crown. But it was the one that depicted a crown hanging from a gallows that held his attention. He immediately thought of the conversation he had overheard in the back room of the inn. It was a guillotine they were talking about, something that would cut off the heads of those who supported the Crown, not hang them, but the object was the same. Then he looked at the sprig of green that some of the marchers were wearing and he thought of the liberty tree, the rebel leader Thomas Archer, and his friend Sammy.

Joshua was thus engaged in his thoughts when he heard a commotion up ahead. The cart came to a stop, and some of those who had got on to it jumped off and made their way forward to see what was happening. Joshua could hear shouting, and, pushing himself up behind Moses, asked him what was wrong.

'It's a minister and some yeomen,' Moses told him. 'He's trying to get them to turn back.'

Through a forest of waving pikes and muskets, Joshua could see a man on horseback. He was dressed in black, and some of the rebels were shouting that he was a magistrate. There was pulling and pushing, the man's horse reared up and he was thrown to the ground. The rebels rushed forward to seize him, there was more scuffling and shouting, and the yeomen turned and galloped off.

Delighted with their capture, the rebels bundled their prisoner on to another cart. Somehow his fall from the horse seemed to underline the vague notion in their minds that everyone would soon be equal. 'Liberty, equality, fraternity,' they chanted and, with guns and spirits high, they made a triumphal entry into the town.

Swept along on the tide of rebellion

Joshua could see that rebels had also marched on the town from other areas and, as they merged, they moved in one great mass down Church Street towards the Market House. He was wondering what to do when shooting broke out somewhere up ahead of them. The marchers immediately stopped and instinctively ducked for cover. There was more shooting, and Joshua could see puffs of smoke coming from windows of the Market House.

In spite of his age, Moses jumped off and was beside them in an instant. 'Get down,' he told them. He lifted Naomi off and whispered to Joshua, 'Hurry! Get away from here as fast as you can.'

'Where to?' asked Joshua. He was crouching beside the cart now, shielding Naomi as best he could. Some of the rebels, he could see, had no weapon at all and were just as scared and confused as they were.

'Anywhere! As long as it's away from here – go on.'

There was more firing from the direction of the Market House and the horse reared up. Several rebels who were still on the cart were thrown to the ground. Others who were crouching near the horse rose to catch it by the bridle, the more immediate danger of being trampled overcoming the fear of being shot.

Grasping Naomi firmly by the hand, Joshua slipped into the nearest alley. In the confusion, only Moses noticed them go, and when he was satisfied that they were out of harm's way he rushed back to help with the horse.

Joshua knew the short cuts through the back yards of the town just as well as he knew the main streets. A few minutes later they emerged out into Mill Street, and with hardly a glance at the Market House, dashed across and ran down the alley to the side door of their father's inn. Pushing Naomi ahead to usher her inside, Joshua glanced back up the alley to make sure no one was following, then tried the door. To his surprise he found it was locked.

'Come on, let's try the front door,' he told her.

They rushed back up the alley only to find that the front

door was also locked.

There was more firing and Joshua looked up at the Market House. He could see the rebels pointing muskets at it from the cover of doors and alleyways and wondered who was inside firing out at them. More importantly, he wondered where his parents were. He pulled Naomi down the side alley again and hammered on the door with his fist. There was still no reply and soon it became obvious that there was no one inside.

'Where's Mammy and Daddy?' cried Naomi. 'Why won't they come to the door?'

'They must be out,' Joshua told her. 'Come on, we'll go up to the loft and wait for Moses. He'll know what to do.'

Lifting Naomi in his arms, he ran down into the stables, and carried her up into the hay-loft. Even there they could hear the shooting at the Market House, interspersed every now and then with the cries and shouts of the rebels.

'Joshua, I'm scared,' said Naomi.

Joshua smiled, and picking a piece of straw from one of her blonde curls, told her, 'You've nothing to be scared about. We're safe in here.'

Below them the horses moved uneasily, and she said, 'I'm scared the moiley cow will get us.'

Joshua took her on his knee and assured her, 'There are no moiley cows in here. That's just the horses you hear.'

'You said the moiley cow was a monster and it would come and eat us all up.'

Joshua laughed. 'I was only joking. I just didn't want you to follow me, that's all. Listen ... see if you can tell me what horse that is, the one directly under us.' In an effort to reassure her and take her mind off what was happening, he continued to talk quietly to her about the horses, naming this one and that one, and as he looked at her little freckled face with its upturned nose, he was sorry that he hadn't been nicer to her the day he and Sammy had gone to Gracehill.

'Joshua, I'm hungry,' she said at last. 'I don't want to

talk about the horses any more. What can we have to eat?'

Joshua was about to reply when he heard a footstep down in the stables. 'Shussh,' he whispered, putting a finger to his lips. They listened for a moment and, when another sound confirmed that there was someone there, Joshua crawled to the edge of the loft and peeped over.

'It's Moses,' he told her. 'Moses, we're up here.'

'Stay where you are,' came the reply, and a moment later Moses joined them.

'There's nobody at home,' Joshua told him.

'And a good thing too,' he replied. 'The town's in the hands of the rebels. All the other inns are closed too, and most of the houses. Everybody's gone.'

'Who's defending the Market House?' asked Joshua.

Moses shook his head. 'I don't know.'

'Moses, I'm hungry,' said Naomi.

Moses took her up in his arms and gave her a hug. 'I'll let you into a little secret,' he told her, 'I'm hungry too.'

'There must be food in the house,' said Joshua. 'I can get in through my window and get it.'

'All right,' said Moses, 'but you'd better hurry. And be careful you can't be seen. It's only a matter of time before that crowd out there get thirsty.'

'You don't think they'd break in, do you?' asked Joshua.

'I don't think it. I know it. They're in control of the town and I can't see this inn, or any of the others, escaping their attention.'

Joshua knew there were thirteen inns in the town; he also knew what drink could do to people and, while he didn't say so in front of Naomi, he reckoned he had better get what food he could and find a safer hiding-place.

None of the rebels had yet tired of the siege of the Market House, and Joshua found the stable yard deserted. Climbing up over the oak casks of whiskey and ale which were stacked against the wall of the outbuildings, he made his way along the thatched roofs to the window of his room. As he climbed in he found himself thinking he was lucky to have a room to himself. It was a luxury not many people of his age had. People like Sammy, for instance. Visions of Sammy's cramped cabin came into his mind. There they all slept in the loft. Then he found himself thinking of the night he saw the outlaws leaving Sammy's house and he tried not to think about him any more.

Quietly he made his way down the stairs. It was strange to see the inn so dark and deserted. Now and then a step creaked, and he stopped, thinking someone might have heard him. But there was no one there. Even the back room where his father and Master Davison and a few other friends talked and drank late into the night was empty.

Several more musket shots stopped Joshua in his tracks. They seemed louder than before, as if they had been fired nearby. They were followed by the sound of footsteps and voices as people ran past the inn. He paused for a moment, half expecting to see the butt of a musket smashing in the front door. The sound of the footsteps receded down the street and he hurried into the kitchen.

Taking a large ashwood bowl, he filled it with anything he could lay his hands on – cakes of oaten bread, cold potatoes which his mother had cooked and abandoned, the remains of a salmon which his father had bought from the fish merchant from Lough Neagh. What else was there? They might get thirsty after eating the fish. Milk? There was no fresh milk, but he found a jug of buttermilk. That was always good for slaking the thirst on a warm day. He squeezed the jug into the bowl beside the rest of the things and, taking care not to spill its contents, hurried back up to his room. By doing a bit of a balancing act he was able to carry the bowl across the low roofs and down over the casks without spilling a drop, and in what seemed to him no time at all – although to Moses it seemed a very long time – he was back up in the hay-loft.

When they had eaten their fill, Joshua persuaded Moses to stay with Naomi while he had a look around for a safer

hiding-place. Moses was strongly opposed to the idea at
first, for they could hear that the battle for the Market
House was still in progress. However, the events of the day
had been a bit much for the old man and, while he
wouldn't admit it, it was obvious he was too tired to go
himself.

'If you went,' said Joshua, 'they might force you to join
them. But nobody's going to pay any attention to someone
of my age, not in these clothes.'

The old man smiled. 'All right. But be careful.'

Joshua promised he would and, telling Naomi he was
going to see if he could find their mother and father, he
climbed down the ladder to the stables and cautiously
made his way out into the street. To his right the battle for
the Market House was reaching a new intensity. He could
smell the smoke from the barrels of the muskets as volley
after volley was exchanged. It lingered in the calm summer
air so that he couldn't see exactly what was going on. Yet
it seemed to him that those who were defending the
Market House had the advantage, as they were firing
down at the rebels who were crouching in doorways. The
smoke smarted in his nose but it was the crack of the
muskets that brought home to him the horrible reality of
what was happening. Somehow he found it difficult to
comprehend that people were actually firing with the
intention of killing each other.

Turning to his left he hurried away, only to find that
within a short distance of the battle there was a distinctly
festive mood in the street. Groups of men were lingering
here and there, peering through the smoke just as he had
done, to see what was going on. Some were armed with
smooth-bladed reaping-hooks and scythes, implements
designed for cutting corn and hay, but of little use in such
a battle. Behind them, others gathered around fires which
they had lit on the street. They had abandoned their
weapons and, it seemed to Joshua, any interest in what
was going on at the Market House. They were talking and

laughing as they cooked food over the open fires and drank from earthenware jugs of whiskey and ale. The drink, he could see, was being brought from a nearby inn; the food was mostly trout and eels, commandeered from the cart of the fish merchant from Lough Neagh.

Pausing beside one group, Joshua heard them talking about how they had captured the magistrate on the march into the town. Recognizing the voice of one of them, he looked up and saw to his surprise that he was a man called Montgomery from Craigbilly on the outskirts of the town, who frequently visited his father's inn. He was boasting about how he had helped to pull the magistrate from his horse, while his nephew smiled and nodded, demonstrating with a kick how he had helped to subdue him.

Whether they had in fact been involved or were just claiming credit for it, Joshua didn't know, but he was afraid they might recognize him and quickly slipped on past. Unknown to him and to the Montgomerys, other ears were also listening. The revellers had forgotten that they were living in a time when Government spies were everywhere. Shadowy figures were watching and waiting for the careless word that would tell the authorities who was doing what and when.

Not knowing where he was going or what he was going to do, Joshua pulled his hat down and with his head lowered hurried on down the street. The United Irishmen were everywhere. Fearing that he might be recognized, he turned down an alley. This took him down into the Shambles, and not wishing to meet Sammy he made his way quickly between the thatched cabins until he reached Bridge Street. It too was crammed. The rebels were milling around, almost as if they had come into the town for market day, and he couldn't help thinking what a strange shape the rebellion had taken.

As Joshua looked around him, he wondered where his parents had taken refuge. He also wondered where on earth he was going to find a safe place for Naomi and

himself to hide. Moses, he could see, was right; it was only
a matter of time before more of the rebels forgot why they
were in town and started looking for drink. The sound of
shooting was still coming from the direction of the Market
House, and he wondered again who was holding out
there. He was turning to go back towards the Shambles
when he saw a familiar face in the crowd. It was Mr Johnston, Sammy's father. So he was still a United Irishman!

Suddenly there was a great surge of rebels down
towards the bridge. Swept along with them, Joshua saw
that the troop of yeomen cavalry had arrived back in the
town after escorting the magistrates to Antrim. Stopping
at the bridge, they sat on their horses, astonished to find
that the town they had left in such a peaceful state was
now crammed with insurgents. For their part, the rebels
were equally surprised by the arrival of the cavalrymen.
For a moment they stood looking at each other, neither
side knowing what to do.

Knowing that there were only sixteen of them, Joshua
was sure the yeomen would turn tail and go for reinforcements. Instead, to his surprise, and the surprise of the
rebels, they moved forward and slowly made their way up
the street. The crowd parted to allow them to pass, but
only until they could surround them. Then, shouting and
yelling, the rebels closed in on them, and Joshua saw the
yeomen being dragged from their horses and disappear
among a forest of pikes.

Within minutes the yeomen had been disarmed and
taken prisoner. Pushing his way out of the crowd, Joshua
ran towards the Shambles and the alley that would take
him back up into the stable yard of his father's inn. He
knew now he must get Naomi and Moses out of there.
They must get away from the inn, away from the town.
Throwing one last look back to make sure no one was
following him, he turned into the alley. As he did so he
crashed into someone, and pulling back in case it was a
rebel he found himself face to face with Sammy.

6

The Battle for the Market House

For a moment, Joshua and Sammy looked at each other. Neither spoke. Somehow time seemed to stand still, each held by his own thoughts and numerous unuttered questions about the other.

After what seemed an eternity, although in reality it was only a split second, Sammy smiled and exclaimed, 'Joshua!'

As if transfixed, Joshua's eyes were still locked with Sammy's. Unable to answer, he made a dash to get past. Even then he was still staring at him, and continued to do so when Sammy put out an arm to stop him.

'Joshua,' said Sammy, 'what's the matter?'

'Your father's a rebel,' stammered Joshua, finding his voice at last.

Sammy shook his head, but before he could deny it Joshua went on, 'I saw them. I saw Archer and the other outlaws at your house.'

'That's right. They were there,' Sammy admitted. 'But not for the reason you think.'

'What else where they doing?' demanded Joshua, 'except visiting another United Irishman?'

'They were there because I made the mistake of telling them where I lived,' said Sammy.

Joshua relaxed. 'What do you mean?'

'That day we met Archer and Dr Lynn and the others in the woods. They asked us who we were. Remember? I told them my father was Nathaniel Johnston, a weaver. I even told them we lived in the Shambles. So, they paid us a visit.'

'What did they want? They didn't think you told on them, did they?'

Sammy shook his head. 'No, but they wanted to know if my father was still a United Irishman, and if not, why not?

My father said he was too busy trying to earn enough to keep his family fed to get mixed up in politics.'

'And what did they say to that?'

'They said that if he joined them there'd be plenty for everybody. They kept talking about liberty and equality and about how everybody would be equal after the rebellion. And they told him not to worry. They'd protect him.' Sammy lowered his head. 'They also made it clear that anybody who wasn't for them was against them.'

'I didn't know that,' said Joshua.

Sammy looked up, as if he had suddenly remembered something. 'But what about you? I didn't expect to find you here with all this going on. I thought you and your family would have got out while the going was good.'

'Well, we tried,' Joshua told him. 'Moses was taking Naomi and myself out to Uncle Matthew's place at Kildowney, but we didn't get far. We met thousands of them marching into town, and they made us turn around and go back with them.'

Sammy smiled. 'There you are then. You were forced to join them too.'

'We didn't exactly join them,' said Joshua. 'I think some of them wanted a lift on the cart more than anything else. When we got in as far as Church Street the shooting started. So we made a run for it.'

'Where did you go?'

Joshua hesitated. For a moment he wondered whether he should disclose their hiding-place. Then, he thought, Sammy was his friend, and he believed what he had told him. 'We're hiding up in the stables,' he said. 'Naomi's there now. Moses is looking after her. When we came back the inn was closed. I don't know where my mother and father are.'

'I don't know if that's a good idea,' said Sammy. 'I mean, hiding in the stables. If they start looking for drink, or horses, it might not be very safe.'

Joshua nodded. 'That's what Moses said. I'm trying to

find somewhere else.'

'Come on,' said Sammy, and hurrying up the alley added, 'I know a place.'

Joshua ran after him and, as they turned into the stables, he asked, 'Where?'

'Our house. Naomi can stay there. You too, if you want.'

Before Joshua could argue, Sammy had climbed up into the loft.

'Did you find Mammy and Daddy?' asked Naomi.

'Not yet,' panted Joshua, 'but don't worry, they'll be back soon.'

'She can stay down at our house until they come back,' Sammy told Moses. 'She'll be safe there.'

'Good idea,' said the old man. 'And what about you, Joshua?'

Sammy smiled. 'He can stay too.' Before Joshua could reply, he added, 'Come on. There's no time to lose.'

Joshua turned to Moses. 'And what about you?'

Moses pushed himself up and put his hands on his hips to ease the aches in his back. 'My place is here with the horses. I'll be all right.'

Knowing how small the weaver's cottage was, and how big his family seemed to be, Joshua couldn't imagine where two more might fit. However, Mrs Johnston soon put him at his ease. Closing both the bottom and top halves of the door, to keep any danger out and her children in, she assured him, 'Don't worry, there's always room for one more.' Seeing Joshua eyeing the loft opposite the fire, she smiled and added, 'Two if need be. There's another loft above the loom and, Sammy, if you move that web of linen there'll be plenty of room.'

Sammy was gone almost before she said it. The younger children were flocking around Naomi, and Joshua could see they were delighted with her. 'Thanks, Mrs Johnston,' he said. 'But I don't want to put you in any danger for sheltering someone like me.'

Worried as she was about what was happening outside, Mrs Johnston smiled again and, looking at his old clothes, said, 'Who's going to know who you are?' She went over to the fire and took the lid off a black pot that hung over it. 'Now, sit yourself down and I'll get you and your sister something to eat.'

Knowing that she had a lot of mouths to feed, Joshua was glad to be able to assure her that Naomi and he had just eaten. 'Well,' she told him as she put the lid back on the pot, 'there'll be a spoonful there, if you want it.'

Apart from four heavy chairs at a table over by the back wall, the only other place to sit was a long bench seat. This was at the foot of a wooden partition that abutted the side of the fireplace and separated it from the doorway of the other room. Some of the Johnston children had now taken Naomi into the other room where, for once, the handloom was idle. Seating himself on the bench, Joshua could hear them playing there, blissfully unaware of the turbulent events that were going on in the streets outside.

Looking up at the loft, he wondered if all the family slept there, or if some of them slept in the loft in the other room. He hoped he wasn't putting any of them out, and he couldn't help thinking how different life must be in the cottage compared with the inn. He could hear the contents of the black pot bubbling away and, even though he was sitting at the end of the bench farthest from the fire, he could feel the heat from the glowing peat.

Behind the fire there was a big black streak on the white wall and occasionally he could smell the soot in the wide chimney above. It was a smell that was in keeping with the rest of the cottage, for overall it had a musty, peaty smell. This, he knew, didn't come entirely from either the fire or the sods of peat on the other side of the hearth, but from the way it was roofed. In contrast to the whiteness of the walls, there were dark brown sods of clay beneath the thatch and, looking up at them, he could see, sticking

through, the white sliced ends of hazel rods, or scallops as
the thatchers called them. The rods, he knew, had been
cut and bent in a U-shape to pin the thatch down.

Joshua was wondering where his parents had gone,
when there was the sound of further shooting up at the
Market House. Mrs Johnston stopped what she was doing
and, looking up, stared in the direction of the shots, as if
she could see it all through the walls. In spite of the brave
face she had put on, she was obviously very agitated by
what was happening and wiping her hands on her apron
she went into the other room to reassure the younger
children. At the same time, Sammy rushed out and, sitting
down beside Joshua, said, 'Did you hear that? They're still
holding out.'

'Who's *in* the Market House?' asked Joshua.

'Master Davison,' Sammy told him. 'And he won't give
up.'

Joshua looked at him in surprise. 'The master? You
mean he's in there on his own?'

'Not at all,' said Sammy. 'He barricaded himself in with
half a dozen of the yeomen cavalry and some others before
the United Irishmen marched into the town.'

Joshua nodded. He remembered the master trying to
rally support at the Market House when they were setting
out for Kildowney. And knowing how strongly Mr Davison felt about the king and the union with Britain, he
wasn't really surprised that he had taken up arms to repel
the rebels. It was then that another thought occurred to
him. 'You don't think my father's in there too, do you?' he
asked.

Sammy shook his head. 'I don't know. I don't think
anybody really knows who's in there, except that they're
being led by Master Davison and he's told the United
Irishmen he'll fight to the last drop of his blood.'

'He will too,' said Joshua. 'I know him.' He gazed into
the glowing peat again, before adding, 'Do you think your
father might know where my parents have gone?'

Sammy looked at him. 'He might. But where are we going to find him?'

'I saw him among the crowd in Bridge Street. You know they seized the rest of the yeomen when they were coming back from Antrim?'

Sammy shook his head. 'No, I didn't. What did they do with them?'

'They pulled them off their horses and took them prisoner.' Joshua got up. 'I'm going to see if I can find out anything.'

Mrs Johnston, who had heard part of the conversation, appeared around the end of the partition. 'I'm sure your parents are all right,' she told him. 'They probably left the town before the United Irishmen arrived and are staying somewhere with friends.'

'Joshua's afraid his father may be helping Master Davison defend the Market House,' Sammy told her.

'I thought maybe Mr Johnston might know where he is,' said Joshua.

Mrs Johnston nodded. 'He might. They forced him to go out there, you know. By right he should be in here working at his loom. He's not cut out to be a rebel.' She sighed and brushed a wisp of hair from her brow with the back of her hand. 'I hope no harm befalls him either.'

'Maybe we could find him,' suggested Sammy. 'Joshua says he saw him in Bridge Street.'

'We'd be very careful,' said Joshua.

Mrs Johnston bit her lip. They could see she was reluctant to let them go, but after a moment's consideration she told them, 'All right. But keep well back from the Market House.'

Unbolting the top half of the door, she peeped out to make sure the way was clear. 'Be very careful,' she whispered, and opening the lower half she let them out.

Behind them they heard the doors being bolted again, and they could see that the doors of all the other cabins were also closed.

'Pull your hair up under your hat,' said Sammy. 'Look, like this. This way we'll draw less attention to ourselves.'

Joshua took his advice and, when he had done so, Sammy smiled and told him, 'Now you look like a croppy!'

It was late in the afternoon now and smoke from the muskets mingled with the darker smoke from the fires that had been lit in the streets. The battle for the Market House had been going on for several hours, and even though the rebels had not succeeded in dislodging the defenders they were in good spirits.

Moving among the crowds that had gathered in Bridge Street, out of range of the muskets, Joshua and Sammy heard the word being passed around that Randalstown was now in the hands of the United Irishmen and that they had gone on to join Henry Joy McCracken in the battle for Antrim town. Someone had it that a force of 10,000 had rallied to McCracken on Donegore Hill and that the garrison in Antrim had been overwhelmed by sheer weight of numbers.

The news spread quickly. It brought wide smiles and loud cheers from section after section of the rebels and, coming so soon after the capture of the sixteen yeomen in Bridge Street, was a source of great assurance, especially to those who dithered on the edges, that they were on the road to victory.

From what they overheard, Joshua and Sammy also gathered that the muskets and ammunition taken from the captured yeomen had been passed up to those who were laying siege to the Market House. So it came as no surprise when, a short time later, a sustained volley of shots signalled a new attack.

However, those inside were not to be dislodged, and from their secure position returned fire with deadly effect. Word now spread that three of the United Irishmen had been shot dead. Surprised and angered, many of the crowd raised their fists and called for vengeance. From the

The battle for the Market House intensifies

direction of Mill Street there were shouts of 'Burn them out,' and Joshua was alarmed to see a flurry of activity which suggested that this was what the rebels were going to do. Others saw it too and, sensing that matters were coming to a head, were pushing and shoving to see what was going to be the outcome.

'Come on, Sammy,' said Joshua. Elbowing their way through the crowd, they made their way back towards the Shambles and up through the alley to Mill Street. Running past the side door of the inn, they saw that the rebels had now opened it up and were helping themselves to jugs of ale and whiskey. However, Joshua's concern was for what was happening up at the Market House, as he now had a strong feeling that his father was among those who were defending it.

Pushing his way up to the front of the crowd, he saw a group of rebels smashing down the gates of the arched doorways of the Market House, and a small flaming tar barrel being taken inside. He turned to say something to Sammy but found they had become separated. He threw another anxious glance at the Market House. The rebels were heaping armfuls of straw on the flaming barrel now and smoke was billowing from the archways. As soon as the straw caught fire, the rebels retreated, and within minutes flames were licking up from the arches.

All the while, other rebels were keeping up a continuous barrage of musket shots. The defenders were shooting back, but now the fire beneath them succeeded in doing what the muskets had failed to do. It forced them to move, and they found they had nowhere to go. The guns fell silent and so did the crowd. Joshua could hear someone shouting to those inside that if they surrendered they wouldn't be harmed. He held his breath and was relieved when, a few minutes later, some of the defenders appeared on the stone steps leading down to the street.

Almost immediately, a section of the crowd rushed forward and the shooting started all over again. It was only a brief exchange of shots, but this time the defenders were caught in the open. To his horror, Joshua saw some of them fall. The others, with the exception of Master Davison, surrendered and were pulled down from the steps. Even then, Master Davison refused to give up, and with his musket empty fought until he was overpowered.

Fearing the worst, Joshua moved forward with the rebels who were jubilant now that they had finally taken control of the town. At the foot of the stone steps they jostled with one another to get a look at the bodies. Joshua recognized one or two of them as local businessmen, but of his father there was no sign.

Feeling a tug on his sleeve, Joshua looked around to find Sammy standing by his side. 'Where have they taken the prisoners?' he whispered.

Sammy shook his head. 'I don't know. Probably into one of the houses.'

There was a crack, and the first floor of the Market House collapsed, sending a shower of sparks out through the nearest archway. Instinctively everyone stepped back and looked up at the building that had been the centre of their struggle for so much of the day. Someone moved them back, saying it was for their own safety, and a short time later carts were brought along the street to remove the bodies.

As the fire in the Market House died down, the spirits of those who had lived to tell the tale rose. Intoxicated by a mixture of drink and jubilation, the streets soon took on a festive atmosphere. All the inns were opened up, the stocks commandeered in the name of the revolution, and liberal supplies of food and drink were distributed among the crowds.

'Any sign of your father?' asked Joshua.

'No, I can't see him anywhere,' Sammy replied.

'Hi, Jackie,' came a voice from the far side of the street, Looking up Joshua saw Timmy Corr and Matty Meek entertaining the rebels. For a moment he feared somebody else might recognize him, but when he remembered that Timmy called everyone Jackie he relaxed and watched their antics.

His head thrown back in typical fashion, Timmy was carrying a broom, while little Matty was trying to shoulder a musket. The musket was twice as long as Matty himself, and lacked the flintlock that would enable it to be fired. But it was plain to see he cared no more about this than Timmy did about his musket being a broom. And so they marched up and down, as proud to be United Irishmen as they had been to be militiamen on another day. Joshua looked at Sammy and smiled. He reckoned they didn't know the difference.

Towards eight o'clock, a man who was obviously a senior rebel leader rode into town at the head of a group of reinforcements. He was an imposing figure in a green uniform and a hat that sported a green cockade. Two pistols were tucked beneath his belt, and a sabre hung by his side. He set up headquarters in an inn on Bridge Street and there held court.

While the fire had destroyed the first floor of the Market House, the tower and other parts of the building were still intact. So also was the dungeon underneath, known as the black hole, and when the flames had died down, the prisoners were put into it. Joshua still didn't know if his father was among them, and, to his horror, he now heard that they were going to be put on trial.

7

A Pocketful of Buttons

Mrs Johnston was right, Joshua thought. No one would know who he was. He was ragged and dirty and his hands and clothes smelled of smoke. He was also itchy and wondered if it was because of something in the old clothes or some bug he had picked up while hiding in the hay above the stables.

He was wandering about the town, hoping against hope that he might see or hear something that would indicate where his parents were. There was general merriment on the streets now, the United Irishmen drinking and eating everything they could find. Some were lying with their shoulders up against the houses, their weapons cast aside, the rebellion as they saw it complete. Others were marching up and down the streets, blowing horns and other instruments in a noisy celebration of their victory.

Stepping over the many rebels who were stretched out on Mill Street, Joshua shrugged his shoulders to ease the itch and scratched his chest, for the itch seemed to be everywhere. And even though he was weighed down with worry about his parents, especially his father, he found himself thinking in a silly sort of way about Jackson's infallible ointment for the itch. Or at least an advertisement in the *News-Letter* said it was infallible: 'It does not contain the least particle of mercury, or any other pernicious ingredient,' it said. 'And it never fails to cure the most desperate case in thirty-six hours, by only twice using.' But then all these things were said to be infallible, he thought. The advertisement under it was for equally infallible rat-powder, but there were still plenty of rats around. Still, he thought, he wouldn't mind some of Jackson's ointment right now, infallible or not.

Joshua's thoughts now returned to his parents. If his

father had joined Master Davison in the Market House, he
reasoned, he would have found a safe hiding-place for his
mother first. He had no doubt about that. But where? And
if his father wasn't among the prisoners in the black hole,
where was he? Unless he was lying dead among the ruins.
If only he could talk to the survivors. At least they could
tell him if his father had been one of them. But the rebels
had mounted a strong guard on the black hole and there
was no way he could get near them.

Joshua was looking across at the remains of the Market
House, when Sammy came running up to him.

'They've got more prisoners,' Sammy shouted above
the din. 'They must have escaped from the Market House
when they set it on fire.'

'Where did they find them?' asked Joshua.

'They've been searching the houses round the back.'

Even as they spoke, the United Irishmen marched their
prisoners up the street. Their clothes were in tatters, their
faces blackened from the smoke and grime and musket-
fire of the day's battle. They were pushed unceremonious-
ly into the already crowded black hole, and Joshua could
see his father wasn't among them. He was wondering what
to do when the rebels began rolling barrels out of a nearby
inn. They placed them in a rectangular pattern where the
streets crossed at the Market House, and then laid planks
across them to make a platform.

Fearing that they might be building a gallows to hang
the prisoners, or even preparing to behead them with the
guillotine he had heard the men talking about in the back
room, Joshua leaned close to Sammy's ear and asked,
'What are they doing?'

Sammy could see the concern in Joshua's face and sense
the alarm in his voice, but, before he could think of
something to say, several of the United leaders came out
of the inn in Bridge Street where they had established
their headquarters, and strode up towards them. Word of
their approach spread quickly, and the crowd fell silent.

'There's Archer,' Joshua whispered.

'And that's one of the sentries who stopped us in the woods that day,' said Sammy. 'Remember, he wanted to let us go.'

Joshua looked around. There was no sign of the tall dark figure of Dr Linn or of the young fair-haired man Brother Fridlezius had identified as Roddy McCorley from Toome. 'I wonder where the others are?' he whispered.

Before Sammy could answer, Archer climbed up on to the makeshift platform, and began to address the crowds that now pushed towards him from all four streets. Speaking at the top of his voice, and walking around so that he faced all of them in turn, he asked them,

'What have you got in your hand?'

'A green bough,' came the reply, those with weapons raising them high.

'Where did it grow?' he asked.

'In America,' they shouted, raising their hands again.

'Where did it bud?'

'In France,' they shouted.

'Where are you going to plant it?' he asked.

'In the Crown of Great Britain,' came a great chorus of reply.

'I think they're talking about the liberty tree,' whispered Joshua.

Sammy nodded. 'Must be some sort of pledge they take.'

Striding around the platform in his green swallow-tailed coat, one hand hovering near his pistols, the other clasping his blunderbuss, Archer was now a striking figure towering above the masses of rebels.

One by one he introduced those who were on the platform with him, describing the younger man, the one they knew as the sentry, as his loyal young captain, John Nevin from Ballymoney. The others lifted their hats to acknowledge the cheers of the crowd, while Nevin's freckled face broke into a wide boyish smile and he waved almost shyly, before dropping his hand to the pommel of his sword.

The introductions over, Archer congratulated their many followers on what he called their great victory. Their comrades, he told them, had taken Randalstown and Antrim and many other parts of the north. The French were on the high seas, sailing at that very moment to give them support. The crowds cheered at this news, and then he told them they'd soon be marching south to join up with the gallant men of Wexford.

Everything Archer said provoked a rousing response. To end his speech, he declared that martial law was over. No more did they have to live in darkness, and he wanted to see a light in every window that night.

On hearing this, some of the rebels hurried off to ensure that his orders were obeyed.

Knowing that his mother and sisters, like the other inhabitants who had remained in town, were sheltering behind closed doors, Sammy said he had better go and make sure they were all right.

Joshua nodded. 'I'll go with you.'

During the night, the flicker of fires could be seen in the distance, as rebels set up outposts on all roads leading into the town. In common with her neighbours, Mrs Johnston put a lighted lamp in the window of her cottage. She also left the top half of the door open, in the belief that the rebels would see them as friends and do them no harm. Now that blood had been spilt, she was clearly very nervous, as there was no knowing where it would all end. Her younger children went to bed with Naomi in the loft opposite the fire, but, between the noise and the excitement of their new-found friendship, they didn't sleep; nor did anyone else.

The rebels continued to celebrate throughout the night. Now and then some of them would walk past the cabin, and occasionally one would lean in over the half door and shout in rebel slogans such as 'Liberty and the green cockade'.

Apart from that, they were left alone, but Mrs Johnston wasn't at all happy with the situation. She spent the night tying her things up in bundles, and vowed that as soon as her husband returned they would be leaving.

The night came and went and still there was no sign of Mr Johnston. Anxious as she was to take her children to safety, Mrs Johnston was reluctant to go without him, and as the morning wore on she asked Joshua if he would go up the street again and see if he could find him.

'I'll go too,' said Sammy, but his mother restrained him.

'No,' she told him. 'I might need you here. If we have to go, I couldn't manage the children by myself.'

Sammy nodded. He realized that in his father's absence his mother was now looking to him for support, and would be happier if he stayed.

She forced a smile. 'Anyway, I'm sure Joshua wants to have another look for his own father.'

If anything, the streets were even more crowded than before, and Joshua reckoned that more contingents of rebels had arrived during the night. Hoping that he might run into Mr Johnston, he made his way along to Bridge Street where he had last seen him. There was no sign of him anywhere, so he decided to search the alleyways behind the Market House. If his father had escaped, he thought, he might still be hiding somewhere at the back. He might even be injured and in need of help. However, the rebels seemed to be everywhere, having taken up quarters in any outhouse or stable they could find, and soon he realized it was futile to continue. He was thinking of returning to Sammy's house when he heard the sounds of voices coming from the inn where the United leaders had set up their headquarters.

A number of rebels were crowding around the back door, craning their necks to see and hear what was going on, while others were using a low roof as a vantage point to look down in through a back window. Wondering if perhaps his father was being held prisoner in the inn,

Joshua climbed up on to the roof and joined the men looking in at the window. 'What's going on?' he panted.

'It's a trial,' one of the men replied.

In the room below, Joshua could see that the rebel leader who had ridden into town the previous evening was sitting at a table on which he had placed his hat with the green cockade and his sword. Before him stood a tall man in a torn shirt and breeches, his hands tied in front of him. For a moment Joshua didn't recognize him. Then he realized it was Constable Crawford. He was strangely unfamiliar without his tall hat and long buttoned coat, but it was him all right.

'What's he supposed to have done?' asked Joshua.

'He's a Government informer,' said one of the men.

Shocked, Joshua wondered if it was because Constable Crawford worked for the Adair estate that the accusation was being made against him. He wanted to tell them that he was really a nice big man and that he had never harmed anybody in his life. But he knew he daren't.

Somebody, he could see, was sitting on a chair as if giving evidence, although what evidence anyone could give against Mr Crawford he couldn't imagine. Nevertheless, the witness was being heard with great interest, and every now and then the crowd in the room would cheer and raise their fists in support of what was being said. When, eventually, the witness had finished, the rebel leader rose and, taking up his sword from the table, walked over to the unfortunate Mr Crawford. Holding the handle of his sword in one hand, the blade in the other, he now addressed him and Joshua reckoned he was informing him of the verdict.

What that was neither Joshua nor the others at the window could hear; nor were they prepared for what happened next. Without warning, the rebel leader took the sword in one hand and plunged it into Constable Crawford. Clutching his stomach, the big man fell to the floor, whereupon the rebel leader raised his sword and finished

The killing of Constable Crawford

him off with a savage blow to the neck.

Joshua gasped and backed away from the window. As he did so, he lost his footing and tumbled to the ground. Numbed, not by the fall but by what he had seen, he picked himself up. The others were laughing and raising clenched fists, and he knew they were laughing not only at him but at the way the man they believed was an informer had been despatched. He felt sick, and holding his hand to his mouth took to his heels. Here and there he stumbled, though over what he did not know, and now and then he banged himself off the narrow walls. But somehow he felt no pain. Nor did he know where he was going; all he knew was that he had to get away.

Finding himself in Bridge Street, Joshua ran up towards the Market House, only to discover that the rebels had dealt a death blow to another of their enemies. This time they hadn't gone through the pretence of a trial, but had dragged the object of their wrath from the black hole. Trembling, he knelt beside the inert body. It was Master Davison. His face was twisted as if from pain, and even though Joshua had often looked at that face with fear and trepidation, he was now filled with a great sense of sadness. Blood, he could see, was still spreading across the once-white shirt, while the black swallow-tailed coat that had so often been tugged at the waist in a gesture of sternness and discipline was soiled and torn. Through his tears he also noted that all the buttons had been torn off. At the same time he heard a tinkle and saw that half a guinea and several buttons had fallen from the pocket of the master's breeches. Surprised, he picked up one of the buttons and looked at it. It bore the letters 'D/C' and he wondered as if in a dream what it all meant.

'Move along there,' someone said gruffly, and Joshua found himself pushed aside by the handle of a pike. The rebels, he realized, must have thought he was going through the pockets of the corpse, and he couldn't help thinking how strange it was that they would take a life but not the worldly goods of their victim.

Afraid now that he might also become a victim, Joshua
picked himself up and ran back down the street. Turning
down an alleyway at the back of the Market House, he ran
as fast as he could towards the Shambles. However, it
seemed to be a nightmare with no end. He hadn't gone far
when he tripped over another body and, thinking it was
one of the rebels who had fallen asleep, he turned to offer
his apologies. Instead, he saw the body of a yeoman, his
arms and legs crumpled and distorted in a way that suggested he had fallen from the Market House.

Unlike the master's coat, the yeoman's tunic had all its
buttons, rows and rows of them, and each bore the letters
'D/C'. Kneeling down, Joshua reached over and, trying
not to look at the face, ran his trembling fingers across the
oval brass badge on the white cross-belt. The badge, he
could see, bore the words, Dunseverick Cavalry. So that's
what the letters meant, he thought – Dunseverick Cavalry.
Taking the button that had fallen from the master's pocket
he held it against one of those on the blood-stained tunic.
They were the same. But why? Why, he wondered, were
there no buttons on the master's coat? And why did he
have a pocketful of yeomen's buttons? Frightened and
confused, he took to his heels again and ran blindly
through the maze of alleyways until he found himself at
Sammy's door.

'Let me in. Let me in,' he cried, banging on the door for
all he was worth.

To his relief, Joshua found that while he himself had
been out Mr Johnston had returned. Still trembling with
shock, he sat down on the bench and, speaking almost
incoherently, tried to tell them about the terrible things he
had seen.

'Constable Crawford,' he said. 'They've killed Constable Crawford. They said he was an informer.'

Mrs Johnston sat down beside him and tried to comfort
him.

'And Master Davison,' he went on. 'He's dead too.'

'Are you sure?' asked Mr Johnston. 'I thought they were holding him prisoner under the Market House.'

'They were,' Joshua continued. 'But they must have taken him out. I saw his body lying on the street. I think they must have piked him. There was blood all over him. And there were buttons in his pocket. Cavalry buttons.'

Thinking that the sight of the bodies had caused Joshua's mind to wander, Mrs Johnston looked at her husband and shook her head.

Realizing that Joshua was in a state of shock, Mr Johnston knelt down beside him. 'It's all right,' he assured him. 'It's all right. Now listen. What's done is done and nobody can undo it. But you have to stop thinking about it. And I've got good news for you. Your father's safe. So's your mother.'

Joshua looked at him. 'Where are they?'

Mrs Johnston squeezed his hand. 'They're out at Gracehill. Your mother's with Sister Hannah, and the brethern are looking after your father.'

'Why, what's the matter with him?'

'He's all right,' said Mr Johnston. 'He was in the Market House, but he escaped. I found him hiding in one of the houses at the back. His left arm stopped a musket ball, but it's nothing serious. Just a flesh wound. I got him out to Gracehill during the night. He'll be safe there.'

Joshua relaxed. 'Thanks, Mr Johnston. I couldn't find him anywhere.'

Mr Johnston nodded. 'But we've got to move. Word's coming in that the attack on Antrim has failed.'

Joshua looked at Sammy. 'I thought they said it was a success? That the town was in the hands of the rebels?'

'That's what they said, all right,' said Sammy.

'They said a lot of things,' Mr Johnston went on. 'But some people have been making their way back from Antrim, and they say things didn't go as planned. Mc-Cracken's men were hoping to seize the magistrates and take the town. But the military were waiting for them.'

'So what do you think we should do?' asked Joshua.

'If the military come, there's no knowing what will happen. I think the best thing we can do is take the children and join your mother and father out at Gracehill. You should all be safe there.'

Joshua managed a smile. 'My father told me he'd find a safe place. That's what the Moravians call it, you know, the Place. But he didn't tell me he wasn't going there himself.'

'Well, he's safe there now,' said Mr Johnston. 'And that's where we're going. We'll carry what we can and take the younger children on our backs.'

Mrs Johnston was already holding two of her children by the hand, anxious to be on her way. Joshua hoisted Naomi on to his back, Sammy and his father did the same with two of the younger children, and off they set.

8

The Black Flies of Lough Neagh

On the gently lapping shore of Lough Neagh, three miles from Antrim town, Shane's Castle glistened brightly in the summer sun. Home of the O'Neills of Clanaboy for at least two centuries, it was built of stone and edged with brick. Over the years the stone had been layered with lime and as a result its whiteness could be seen for miles around, shining like a beacon across the calm waters of the lough.

On one of its turretted towers, the flag of the O'Neills fluttered high above the lake and its ancient oak woods, a flag conspicuous for the crimson splash at its centre – the red hand which was the main feature of the O'Neill coat of arms.

It was said that in times gone by a young Scandanavian called Niel had won the land of Ulster for himself by cutting off his right hand and throwing it on to the shore. In time the bloodied hand was to become the emblem of the O'Neills and of Ulster.

Now, many centuries later, the United Irishmen had tried to secure the land of Ulster and, in the process, the blood of the O'Neills had been spilt again. Indeed, a lot of blood had been spilt.

Having received advance information from their spies, the military had been ready at Antrim, and even though the United Irishmen had converged on the town in great numbers they were no match for trained soldiers. At the end of the day, they had dispersed in disarray, leaving upwards of three hundred dead and wounded behind.

Satisfied that the town was now secure, a group of officers rode up the driveway to Shane's Castle and dismounted beneath one of the large oak trees. As they walked up to the doorway, their leader, Colonel Clavering,

looked up at the flag. Lord O'Neill had been seriously
wounded at the battle of Antrim, and soon, he knew, the
flag would be flying at half mast.

Inside the officers were met by Lord O'Neill's wife and
their nineteen-year-old son, Charles. On the walls around
them hung paintings of the long line of O'Neills, including
John, the 1st Viscount, who now lay dying from a pike
wound. According to one account, he had arrived at
Antrim from Dublin as the military confronted the insurgents and had positioned himself near the courthouse when
a man in a grey frieze coat rushed forward. He had turned
his horse several times, it was said, in an attempt to ward
off his assailant and fired his pistol, but had been brought
to the ground by a thrust of a pike to his side. Gravely
wounded, he had been taken down the river by boat and
across the bay to the castle where he now lay.

Colonel Clavering shook hands with Lady O'Neill, then
with her son, and expressed the hope that Lord O'Neill
would soon recover. Inviting them to sit down, Lady
O'Neill did likewise, and dabbed the tears from her swollen
eyes. Even in her grief, they could see that her reputation as
a woman of exceptional beauty had not been exaggerated.

'I don't understand,' she said. 'I mean, for years John
has worked hard in the Irish Parliament to ensure that Ireland received proper treatment. He has also supported
Catholic emancipation.'

The colonel nodded. In his view it was the agitation for
Catholic emancipation and other reforms that had led to
the rebellion.

Young Charles, who was heir to the title, comforted his
mother, and asked the colonel, 'Is it true he was caught
between the opposing sides? We have received certain
indications of regret.'

In fact, Colonel Clavering had heard several accounts of
how Lord O'Neill had been wounded and why. One of
these suggested that it might have been an act of revenge,
as the removal of tenants from the estate over the years to

Colonel Clavering at Shane's Castle

facilitate landscaping had caused a lot of ill feeling. Some prisoners, on the other hand, were saying that the pike-man had merely acted in self-defence, after his lordship had fired at him.

Whatever the truth of it, and not wishing to offend the family by referring to the first story, Colonel Clavering told them, 'One of our prisoners has claimed that they would have let him pass had he not fired at them. But the fact is, it was the thrust of a pike that laid him low. And be assured, they will pay for it this day. They will pay dearly for all the actions they have taken against the Crown.'

Lord O'Neill being the governor of the county, Colonel Clavering considered it only natural that Shane's Castle should be his headquarters, and it had been agreed that they would use a drawing-room in the west wing for that purpose.

As his officers spread a large map on the table, Colonel Clavering stood at a window looking out over the lough. He could see the tufted head of a great crested grebe float-ing on the ripples, not far from the shore, while another bird like a white swallow patrolled the shallows, diving occasionally for small fish. Had he known it, this black-headed bird was a common tern, whose forked tail and graceful flight and earned it the name of sea-swallow.

However, there was no room for the niceties of nature in the military mind of Colonel Clavering. Instead, he was thinking of the many midges that had dropped from the trees to torment himself and his men, and their horses, as they had cantered up the driveway. Above the tree-lined shore he could now see dark swarms of midges. On a previous visit, Lord O'Neill had told him they were the famous black flies of Lough Neagh. A bit of a nuisance his lordship had said, but they laid their eggs on the surface of the lough, thus providing a ready source of food for fish.

Needless to say, the mating habits of the black flies of Lough Neagh were of no interest to the colonel either. But he did remember Lord O'Neill saying that some of the adults – he couldn't recall if it was the males or females – only lived a few days. Now, as he looked at them, they reminded him of the swarms of insurgents who had laid siege to the towns around him. Every rebel that could be found had been hunted down and shot, and he promised himself that, like the midges, the lives of their leaders would also be short.

As if reading his mind, one of his officers told him, 'The leaders of the assault on Antrim have fled to Slemish. We have information that McCracken tried to rally his men again at Donegore Hill, but didn't succeed.'

Colonel Clavering was still looking out through the window, his hands clasped behind his back. 'Well, he won't find much comfort on the mountain. Sooner or later he'll have to come down, and when he does he'll hang.'

'Randalstown and Ballymena are still in the hands of the rebels,' he was told.

The colonel, who was still watching the swarms of midges, nodded and, without turning round, said, 'Right then. Issue this proclamation. Tell the rebels at Randalstown that if their arms are given up I will grant protection to the people, and there will be a complete amnesty. If not, I will put every man, woman and child to the sword and burn their dwellings.'

The other officers looked at each other, and one asked by way of confirmation, 'A complete amnesty, provided they hand up their weapons?'

'Correct. Then they must hand over their leaders.'

'And if they don't?'

'If they don't, burn the town.'

'And Ballymena?' asked the other officer.

Colonel Clavering turned and assured him, 'I'll deal with Ballymena when the time comes.'

Having set out for Gracehill on foot, Joshua and the Johnstons found that many other stragglers had also taken to the road, but where they were heading perhaps they themselves did not even know.

As they approached a rebel outpost at the edge of the town, Mr Johnston surprised everyone by calling out, 'Fitzgerald in the dark!'

The rebels laughed and let them through.

'Nathaniel,' said his wife almost accusingly. 'What do you mean, "Fitzgerald in the dark"?'

'It was all I could think of,' her husband replied. They said that would be the password. I suppose it was meant for night-time.'

'What does it mean?' asked Sammy.

'Lord Edward Fitzgerald,' his father told him. 'He was their leader in Dublin. He was arrested before the rebellion broke out.'

As they crossed the river, the bell of the newly erected clock tower on the church at Gracehill marked the hour, and somehow Joshua felt as if it was calling them to safety. When they arrived in the square they found that many other families, mostly supporters of the Crown, had also sought refuge, and the square, which was usually neat and tidy, was now littered with carts and bundles of clothing.

Joshua let Naomi slip down his back to the ground and, hunkering down told her, 'This is where Mammy and Daddy are.'

He straightened up, and Mr Johnston said, 'I left your father with Brother Fridlezius, but I don't know where your mother is.'

'She knows Sister Hannah,' said Joshua. 'She's probably with her. She lives in the single sisters' house.' He looked at Mrs Johnston. 'Maybe if you took Naomi and the girls there, Mrs Johnston, I could look for Brother Fridlezius and find out where my father is.'

'Good idea,' said Mr Johnston. 'And Sammy, you come with me. We'll go down to the inn. Maybe somebody there can tell us what's going on in the rest of the country.'

Mrs Johnston looked at her husband in a way that suggested that she was wondering whether he was proposing to go to the inn for news or for drink. But before she could put the question into words, they heard the sound of pounding hooves and saw eight yeomen galloping into the square. Stones flew up from the dusty street as they spurred their mounts around the corner. They had two riderless horses in tow, and the neck of one of these was saturated with blood.

Instinctively everyone took cover behind the carts. At the bottom end of the square, the yeomen pulled savagely on the reins to bring their mounts skidding to a halt outside the inn. The horses were in a lather from being ridden so hard. Their eyes were bulging, their nostrils flared, and they snorted and threw up their heads to free themselves from the tugging reins.

'There's Brother Fridlezius,' whispered Joshua.

Anxious to see what all the commotion was about, Brother Fridlezius was hurrying over from a nearby house. The brother in charge of the inn had also come to the door, but the yeomen didn't dismount. Stopping only long enough to exchange a few words, the soldiers handed them the reins of the riderless horses and galloped off again in a shower of dust and stones.

Before the dust had time to settle, the two brethren gave an anxious look around. Then, taking the horses by the bridles, they ran with them as fast as they could along the bottom of the square and up the far side.

'They're taking them into the stables at the back of the church,' said Joshua. 'Come on.'

'Right,' said Mr Johnston. All thoughts of the inn now forgotten, he helped his wife to take the children over to the single sisters' house and, leaving them at the door, hurried after Joshua and Sammy.

In the yard behind the warden's house, the boys found that several other brethren had now appeared to help calm the two horses. Speaking to them in soothing tones, they patted them and began rubbing them down with handfuls of straw. Brother Fridlezius was concerned about the

wound one of the horses had on its neck, and when it had
settled down he tried to staunch the flow of blood. Putting
an arm under and around to pat the other side of its neck,
he began rubbing off the blood below the wound. In this
way he gradually worked his way up to the wound itself.
At first the horse threw back its head and reared up, but
bit by bit he gained its confidence and eventually succeeded in covering the gash with a piece of cloth he had
smeared with liniment.

'They said it was a thrust of a pike,' he said to no one in
particular. The others watched him smooth the edges of
the cloth to try and make it stay on. Another of the
brethren was holding the horse by the bridle and, almost
as if it knew it was being helped it was now standing re-
markably still, only an occasional tremble of its neck skin
betraying its discomfort. 'During the battle of Antrim,' he
continued, 'the rider of the other horse was shot.'

'What news did they bring from Antrim?' asked Mr
Johnston.

'The United Irishmen were driven out with heavy
losses,' Brother Fridlezius replied. 'Bodies of men and
horses are lying in the streets and fields. The rebel leaders
are on the run – McCracken, McCorley and a whole lot
more.' One of the brethren gave him another cloth and he
wiped the blood off his hands. 'They also brought news
that Lord O'Neill has been badly wounded.'

'Master Davison's been killed,' Joshua told him. 'And
Constable Crawford. It just happened this morning.'

'Ballymena's still in the hands of the rebels,' added Mr
Johnston.

Brother Fridlezius nodded. They could see that he was
shocked by the news that blood had now been spilt nearer
home, the blood of people he probably knew.

'Mr Johnston said my father was wounded,' said Joshua.
'Is he all right?'

'He's fine,' Brother Fridlezius assured him. 'We've
hidden him in one of the labourers' cottages.' Seeing that

they didn't understand, he explained, 'You see, it's not safe for outsiders to be seen here – the menfolk, I mean. The rebels have threatened us with destruction if we harbour supporters of the Crown, and the yeomen have warned us not to harbour rebels. The rebels have even threatened us for not joining them.'

'The United Irishmen were here again at four o'clock this morning,' said one of the other brethren. 'Marched into our Place with pikes, guns, pistols, swords and scythes affixed to long poles. And they had green flags.'

'They were looking for guns,' Brother Fridlezius added, 'but they left when we told them we hadn't got any. They said their committee had decided that no harm would be done to our Place, but you never know. The situation changes by the hour and with every party that marches through.'

'What do you think we should do?' asked Mr Johnston. 'My wife and children have gone to the single sisters' house.'

'Looking for Sister Hannah and my mother,' added Joshua.

Brother Fridlezius nodded. 'Good. They'll find her safe and well, and Sister Hannah will see that they're taken care of too. But ...' He eyed them up and down. 'It wouldn't be easy to convince the yeomen or the United Irishmen that you're not rebels who have fled the town. And in either event you'd be in serious trouble. Come on. I'll find you somewhere to hide. When darkness comes I'll take you to see Mr Watson.'

The Moravian brethren were renowned for the quality of the linen they produced, and for the past two years had been involved in every stage of its production, from the extraction of the thread from the flax to the weaving and whitening of the cloth.

It seemed natural to Brother Fridlezius then that the best way to hide a weaver was to put him and his two helpers to work in the weaving shed. Whatever about Sammy, Joshua would have preferred to help Brother Fridlezius with his wood-carving. However, he accepted that they would be less conspicuous if they joined those toiling in various dusty corners of the shed to feed the handlooms.

During the afternoon, they watched anxiously as a party of United Irishmen marched into the settlement. They had a prisoner with them, a wounded yeoman. He could hardly walk and, after some discussion, they decided to leave him at the inn. When they had gone, Brother Fridlezius reported that they had given an assurance that no one at the settlement would be harmed. This gave Joshua and his friends some comfort, but still they were advised not to venture out until after nightfall.

It seemed an age before the sun began to sink beyond Lough Neagh, and even longer before Brother Fridlezius called again. Darkness had come, but it had the thinness of summer about it. As a result Joshua and his friends could clearly see the outline of the square and surrounding village as Brother Fridlezius led them up to the warden's house. Quietly they made their way past the darkened church and over to the single sisters' house where Joshua was reunited with his mother.

Mrs Watson was having a sip of tea, real tea as she called it, with Sister Hannah and putting it aside, she got up, exclaiming, 'Joshua! Look at you. The dirt!'

Joshua took off his hat and not quite knowing what to say, scratched his ribs.

'And I hope you haven't got fleas,' she added with not a little consternation.

It was typical of his mother, he thought, that she should greet him with such a remark, and he would have been embarrassed had Sammy been listening. However, he could see that Sammy and his father were busy talking to their own family. So he just smiled, and said, 'They're the old clothes you made me wear yesterday.'

'Yesterday,' said his mother. 'It seems like an eternity since you and Naomi set off with Moses. Come here 'till I have a better look at you.'

So saying, she tried to wipe the dirt off his face with her hand, then embraced him in a way that said, dirty or not, she was delighted to see him. This really did embarrass him, and when, a few moments later, Brother Fridlezius suggested they had better be going, he rammed his hat back on his head and was first out through the door.

Leaving the square, Brother Fridlezius led the three of them out to the farm, and there, in one of the labourers' cottages, they found Mr Watson resting on a bed. Seeing that he had his arm in a sling, Joshua asked him how he was.

'I'm fine, I'm fine,' his father assured him, and flexed his fingers to demonstrate that the wound wasn't serious. 'Here,' he added, moving over to make room, 'sit down beside me and tell me what's been happening. Brother Fridlezius tells me Master Davison is dead. How can that be? I thought he was taken prisoner.'

'He *was* taken prisoner,' Sammy informed him.

'But they must have dragged him out during the night,' said Joshua. 'I think they piked him to death.'

'He vowed he wouldn't give in, that he would fight to the bitter end,' recalled Mr Watson.

'He did that all right,' affirmed Mr Johnston.

'He even took the buttons from his coat and fired those,' said Mr Watson. 'And when they were gone he got some from the yeomen.'

Joshua took out the cavalry button that had fallen from the master's pocket. 'You mean, he used buttons for ammunition? But sure they wouldn't have much effect.'

'Not on their own,' his father agreed. 'But he also used nails, iron pegs, anything he could find. That way he was able to make his real ammunition last longer. He reckoned the longer we could hold out, the more hope there was that the military might come to our aid.' He sighed. 'But, it wasn't to be.'

'And who else was in the Market House?' asked Joshua.

As his father went over the names of the others, Joshua recognized two of them as Catholics and thought what a strange rebellion it was.

'How did you get out?' asked Sammy.

'Well, I was wounded in the arm. Master Davison insisted that myself and a few others – he talked about families and that sort of thing – he insisted that we should get out while the going was good. So we made our way into the adjoining buildings. Later I heard the rebels searching for us. Some of the others were discovered and taken prisoner. They would probably have found me too eventually, but during the night your father located me and brought me out here.' Mr Watson turned to Joshua. 'But tell me, is it true about Constable Crawford?'

Joshua nodded, and told him how the rebel leader had cut the constable down with his sword.

Mr Watson sighed. 'Poor man.'

'The United Irishmen are still in control of the town,' said Mr Johnston. 'But we hear they've been defeated at Antrim.'

'Eight yeomen came into our Place today,' said Brother Fridlezius. 'They told me the rebels were driven out of Antrim with heavy losses. Randalstown's next, they said. Then Ballymena.'

'What else did they say about Ballymena?' asked Mr. Watson.

'They left a message for the rebels. They said we were to tell them that if they didn't surrender, they'd reduce the town to ashes.'

The message, it transpired, was no idle threat. The following morning a pall of black smoke was seen rising slowly into the sky, and even though it was eight miles away everyone in the district knew Randalstown was in flames. Word spread that the rebels there had agreed to surrender their weapons but not their leaders, with the result that the houses had been put to the torch. Soon smoke was seen rising in other parts of the district, and fearing that the king's army was now marching on Ballymena, the families of those who were loyal and those who were not fled to Gracehill. By Sunday morning, every house in the settlement was full of refugees, while many others were camped in the village square with their bundles of belongings.

With the fear of vengeance now upon them, people of all denominations – Catholics, Protestants and Dissenters – crowded into the small church with the Moravians. For once all religious and political differences were set aside, and that evening Joshua watched Brother Fridlezius record the event in the settlement's diary. 'They bowed the knee,' he wrote, 'and joined heartily together in deep devotion and worship to the God and Father of them all.'

No one, not even Brother Fridlezius, could have imagined how much more would be required of them before it was all over.

9

The Flogging Field

Rooks were swirling above the woods of the Adair demesne like dark clouds gathering in a sunny sky. Beneath them, Sammy and Joshua ran through the trees for all they were worth, just as they had done on another sunny day a long time ago, before all the trouble had begun. This time they weren't racing each other, but trying to get ahead of a column of Government troops which had marched up through the town.

When they reached the field inside the entrance they were in time to see several hundred bayonets flashing in the sun, as the troops, who had lined up in long rows, shouldered their muskets.

'Quick,' whispered Joshua, 'give me a leg up.'

Sammy helped Joshua climb into the nearest tree and was in turn pulled up after him. From their vantage point, they now had a panoramic view of the assembled troops. Some, they could see, were regular soldiers from England, others members of the Monaghan Militia. All wore bright red tunics, and as he looked down on them Joshua couldn't help thinking that the tunics were like stains of blood on the green of the grass. Perhaps it was because he was thinking of Constable Crawford and how he would have come out of the porter's lodge to let the troops in. Maybe it was because he had been thinking of Master Davison and how he himself would have been at school now that it was Monday morning, if the master had been alive. Or perhaps it was the thought of the dead yeoman he had fallen over behind the Market House. He wasn't sure but, whatever it was, the red tunics reminded him of the colour of blood.

In front of the troops, several officers sat astride their horses, some of which bowed and pranced as the last of

Joshua and Sammy watch the troops assemble

the troops moved into position. From the handles of their sabres hung gold and silver tassels which rolled with the movement of the horses and, like the bayonets, glinted whenever they caught a ray of sun. Only a few days before, the same tassels had been wrapped around their wrists to ensure that the swords would stay in their hands as they slashed at the rebels in Antrim town. But for now the swords were in their scabbards, the tassels an impressive decoration.

Sammy and Joshua had left Gracehill with their parents when word had arrived that those inhabitants of Ballymena who didn't return would be regarded as rebels and their houses burned. The rebels, they found, had lost all heart for the fight when news of the defeat at Antrim had reached them, and when Government troops had appeared on the hills they had melted back into the countryside, leaving the townspeople to face the wrath of the army.

'There's my father,' said Joshua.

A group of people had now entered the demesne and were walking over to the officers who were still on horseback. Besides Mr Watson, they could see that the deputation included other people of some standing in the town.

'I wonder what they're saying?' said Sammy.

'I don't know,' Joshua replied. 'But whatever it is, my father doesn't look very pleased about it.'

A few moments later the deputation turned and walked away. The officers waited until they had gone out through the gates, then brought their horses round to face their men. With shouted orders, the soldiers were dismissed, and Sammy whispered, 'Come on. We'd better get out of here. If they spot us, they might think we're spying on them. And you heard what happened to the weaver's son in Randalstown.'

Joshua nodded. They had heard that several people, including a boy their own age, had been shot and killed during house searches in Randalstown. There was no way of knowing if it was true, but now, as some of the soldiers began to wander close to the tree where they were hiding, they scrambled down as fast as they could, and made a beeline for the boundary wall.

When they returned to the inn, they found Mr Watson helping Moses to load provisions on to the cart in the stable yard.

'What's happening?' panted Joshua.

Mr Watson wiped the sweat from his brow with his fore-arm. His other arm was still in a sling. 'Colonel Clavering has demanded that we provide his troops with food and drink.'

'Here, we'll do that,' said Sammy, and the two of them helped Moses to lift a bag of flour up on to the cart.

'But sure there's hardly anything left,' said Joshua. 'The rebels have taken most of it.'

'We've no choice,' his father explained. 'Either we give them what we have, or they come and take it.'

'But what about the amnesty?' asked Joshua.

'It's the United Irishmen who are getting the amnesty,' said Mr. Watson. 'All we're getting is the blame.'

'Do you mean they're all getting off scot-free?' asked Sammy.

'Not all of them,' said Moses.

'The amnesty doesn't apply to the leaders,' said Mr Watson. 'Or, I would imagine, to anyone else they can prove was involved. They're setting up their headquarters in Castle Street. All offenders will be tried by military court.'

'What does that mean?' asked Joshua.

'It means,' his father told him, 'that they're going to hang them.'

'But how will they know who was involved?' asked Sammy.

'The United Irishmen weren't the only ones in town,' said Moses. He pushed the bag of flour into place on the cart, and added, 'You can rest assured the Government had their spies here too.'

'They're probably drawing up a list of troublemakers at this very moment,' said Mr. Watson. 'And all I can say is, God help them.'

Within hours, Colonel Clavering had set up his head-quarters in the premises in Castle Street used by the yeomen and, as if to add insult to injury, his troops installed themselves in the town's two places of worship – the parish church in Church Street, and the Presbyterian meeting-house. Then, acting on the information of their spies, the troops moved into action.

Sammy's father had returned to his loom and, after a long day's work, had gone to bed with his family in the loft opposite the fire. He was happy to be back at work, and was thinking that weaving was much more to his liking than rebellion when there was loud hammering on the cabin door.

'All right, all right,' he shouted. 'I'm coming.'

His wife sat up and watched him climb down the ladder to open the door. 'Be careful, Nathaniel,' she whispered. 'You wouldn't know who's abroad these nights.'

Sammy, too, was sitting up. The rebel leaders were still at large and he feared it might be Archer and Dr Linn, calling again to punish his father for not taking an active part in the rebellion.

No sooner had Mr Johnston unbolted the top half of the door than it was flung back, and several bayonets were thrust in at his throat. A militiaman reached in to unbolt the lower half, and before he knew what was happening they had pushed in on top of him.

Seeing her husband lying on the floor, a hand raised to try and protect himself from the sharp points of the bayonets, Mrs Johnston screamed. A militiaman immed-iately climbed the ladder and threw back the clothes to see who else might be there. Now awake, the children also screamed, and Sammy shouted, 'There's no one else here, only the children.'

'You,' said the militiaman, pointing his bayonet at Sammy. 'You come down here too.'

Mrs Johnston pleaded, but her cries, like those of her children, were in vain. Sammy and his father were allowed to delay only long enough to pull on their breeches before they were marched out into the night.

By morning it became clear that Mr Johnston had been on a very long list of names supplied to the military by Government spies. Many other cabins had been raided during the night and the menfolk arrested. Some cabins in outlying areas had also been burned. As a result, Mrs Johnston was only one of a number of women who came to the inn, seeking the help of Mr Watson in locating their husbands and sons.

There was a crack of a whip, and a sharp intake of breath from those who watched, as the leather thong lashed the frail body of Samuel Bones. Attracted by the freshly spilt blood, a fly landed on the crimson streak, only to be squashed by the next lash and disappear as streak was laid upon streak. The thin line of men, women and children who watched did so, not out of morbid curiosity, but because of the sharp pointed bayonets that were levelled at their backs.

'What's going on here?' asked Mr Watson.

Having been told at Castle Street that Colonel Clavering had gone to Broughshane, Mr Watson had got Moses to saddle his horse and, with Joshua clinging on behind, had ridden the three miles to the village in the hope of finding him. In a field called the Fir Park he had spotted the red coats of the military, and found that punishment was already being meted out to those who had been arrested.

One of the soldiers turned and, raising his musket, prodded Mr Watson on the chest with the point of the bayonet. 'Come to see the flogging then?' he smiled.

Joshua, who had his arms around his father, pulled his

hands back out of the way. The soldier, he could see, was a regular from England.

'I've come to see Colonel Clavering,' replied Mr Watson.

The soldier was now eyeing Mr Watson's injured arm, probably wondering if he had stopped a musket ball in the recent fighting and on what side he had been when he had done so. 'And what would the likes of you be wanting with the colonel?' he asked.

'That's my business,' asserted Mr Watson.

'Well, what you do here is my business,' grinned the soldier. 'You see, our orders – orders from the colonel that is – say that everyone here must watch the flogging.'

'But I'm not from here,' protested Mr Watson. 'I'm from Ballymena, and I've come to see the colonel.'

'That's as may be,' said the soldier, 'but you're here now, and you must watch with the rest of them.'

Realizing it was useless to argue, Mr Watson replied, 'Very well, but I must warn you. I'm acquainted with Colonel Clavering and, if you fail to inform him that I have come to see him, you must bear the consequences.'

Not the least bit impressed, the soldier caught the horse by the bridle and was ordering them to dismount, when an officer arrived and inquired what was going on.

'I wish to see Colonel Clavering,' Mr Watson told him.

Thankfully the officer was more observant than the soldier. He could see from the way Mr Watson was dressed that he was a person of some substance; even the fact that he was on horseback showed clearly that he wasn't a peasant. 'And what name will I say?'

'Mr Watson. I'm an innkeeper from Ballymena.'

'And tell me, innkeeper,' said the officer. 'How did you come by your injury?'

'In the battle for the Market House.'

'Inside, I trust?'

Mr Watson nodded, and the officer replied, 'All right, wait here.'

Joshua and his father watched as Samuel Bones received the remainder of his punishment, and when his bloodied body was dragged away Mr Watson inquired, 'How many lashes did he get?'

'Five hundred,' a soldier replied. 'Two hundred and fifty on the back, same on the buttocks.'

A man called Samual Crawford was next. Someone said he was from Ballymena, although Joshua didn't recognize him. He too had been ordered to receive five hundred lashes, and soon his body began to sag under the onslaught of the whip. 'Gentlemen, be pleased to shoot me,' was all he said, but the soldiers didn't oblige. Taking turns, for it was tiring work, they administered the punishment to the very last lash.

As if to cool all concerned, a summer shower now swept the Fir Park, but it was of little comfort to the next victim of the military's punishment. A young man by the name of Hood Haslet was tied to the whipping post. Joshua knew him to see and reckoned he wasn't any more than nineteen. His punishment was also five hundred lashes. The rain added to the sting of the lash, and he was heard to say, 'I'm a-cutting through.' By that stage he had only received a hundred lashes, and Joshua was thankful to see the officer returning, for he knew he couldn't watch any more.

'The colonel is busy at the moment,' the officer informed his father. 'But he will be pleased to see you tomorrow morning in Castle Street, at his headquarters.'

Mr Watson thanked him and, telling Joshua to hold on, turned his horse around and headed for home. Soon the sounds of whipping and sobbing were left behind, but even then neither spoke. Both were shocked by what they had seen and fearful that Sammy and his father might suffer the same fate – or worse – before they could intervene.

Soldiers were busy nailing posters to every door in the town when Joshua and his father returned to Ballymena.

Mr Watson pulled up before he entered the stable yard
so that he could have a look at them. 'They're reward
posters,' he announced.

'Who for?' asked Joshua, who was trying to see around
him.

'For the leaders of the rebellion, who else.'

Sliding to the ground, Joshua rushed over to see
for himself what the posters had to say, and found that
they offered rewards for information leading to the capture
of those who had led the rebellion in Antrim and neighbouring areas. Chief among them was Henry Joy Mc-
Cracken; also several people called Orr, who were wanted
for the attack on Antrim town. But of more interest to him
were the names he knew – Dr Linn of Randalstown,
Roddy McCorley of Toome and Thomas Archer of Ballymena.

It was no surprise, therefore, that when Joshua and his
father called at the army's headquarters in Castle Street
next day Colonel Clavering should be demanding the
arrest of the very same people.

They had been told to wait, and were sitting on a bench
outside his door when a shaggy brown dog trotted in and
sniffed around their feet.

'Hello, boy,' said Joshua, patting it on the head. 'What's
your name, then?' The dog licked his hand and he asked
his father, 'What sort is he?'

'I think he's a water-spaniel,' his father replied.

'I'm not surprised,' said Joshua. 'Look at the state of
him. He must have been rooting around in the river. I
wonder who he belongs to?'

Before his father could answer, Joshua heard a raised
voice coming from the room. They both stopped talking
to hear what the colonel was saying, for he was telling
someone in no uncertain terms that he wanted the liberty
tree destroyed.

'It's not enough,' he thundered, 'that it should be
stripped of its leaves, or even its branches. It must be torn

up by the root – and that means finding the leaders of this uprising. McCracken won't last long on the slopes of Slemish – we'll soon hunt him down. But Archer and his band – they're the ones who held this town to ransom. They must be brought to justice, and that, Captain Dickey, will be your job.'

Several soldiers came in and the noise they made as they stacked their weapons drowned out whatever else was said. A few minutes later, a young orderly came to the door and invited Joshua and his father in. To their surprise, the dog squeezed in alongside them and, throwing itself down on the floor, began scratching itself.

Colonel Clavering and the man he had been talking to were in their shirt sleeves and breeches, and Joshua got the impression that while it was another warm day, it was in the heat of the discussion about Archer and his men that they had discarded their tunics.

'Ah, Mr Watson,' said the colonel and, gesturing with a hand towards the other man, added, 'This is Captain Dickey of Hillhead. He's in charge of the yeomen now.'

It was the first time Joshua had seen Colonel Clavering at close quarters, and somehow he felt frightened of him. A tall powerful figure, he paced the floor, his fist pounding his hand behind his back in a way that suggested he had little time for handshakes and was impatient to get things done. But it was his face that frightened Joshua most; it was long and bony, the eyes were a distant grey, the expression humourless and unforgiving. Here, he knew, was a man with the power to flog, transport or hang, and the look in his eyes said he would never flinch from doing so.

Mr Watson already knew Captain Dickey and, when he had shaken hands with him and introduced Joshua, Colonel Clavering sat on the edge of the desk. 'I've just been telling Captain Dickey,' he continued, 'that the district won't be entirely secure until we apprehend the leaders of this uprising. In particular, that deserter and brigand, Thomas Archer.'

Mr Watson nodded and, as they got down to business, Joshua could see that Captain Dickey was shorter, fatter, less fit than the colonel and had a redness about his face that indicated a more comfortable way of living. The water-spaniel was now lying at his feet and was obviously his. Somehow its presence suggested that he might be more at home cantering around his estate on one of his horses or strolling through the woods with dog and gun. But for now he was fulfilling his other role, for it was members of the landed gentry like him who commanded the part-time soldiers of the yeomanry corps.

Joshua looked around for his tunic to see if it was the dark blue of the yeomen cavalry or the bright red of the infantry. There was no sign of it, and he reckoned the young orderly had put it away somewhere. Anyway, he thought, Captain Dickey didn't look the sort of man who would be walking with the infantry. Blue coat or red, he would be on a horse. Of that he had no doubt.

Now, as he listened, Joshua thought of the day he and his friend Sammy had contemplated a raid on the orchard in the Dickey estate. And he wondered what would have happened to them if they had raided it and if they had been caught. They had climbed over the wall of the estate, which was a short distance north of the town, and were thinking how tempting the apples looked. But then they had remembered what happened to people who were convicted of theft – even people who stole relatively small things, such as a piece of cheese, a pair of shoes or a length of cloth. They were transported to a faraway place with the fearful name of Van Diemen's Land, or to New South Wales, which by all accounts was equally far away.

Sammy's father, who as a weaver was very conscious of the value of cloth, often spoke of a young woman called Bridget McDonnell who had been sentenced to death for the theft of eleven yards of cotton from a shop in Armagh. She was later reprieved and ordered to be transported for life. It was said she was taken to the Cove of Cork with her year-old daughter and put on board the *Queen*, the first convict ship to sail directly from Ireland to New South Wales.

Thoughts of transportation hadn't prevented some of the rebels from climbing over the wall during the rebellion and raiding Captain Dickey's wine cellars. Some of the womenfolk, it was said, had also bickered among themselves over who should become the new lady of the manor. Yet, strange as it may seem, the rebels had laid no serious claim to the estate. Nor had they laid claim to the Adair demesne. It was, Joshua heard his father observe, as if they really had no clear idea what their action was supposed to achieve, apart from taking over the town by sheer weight of numbers.

Nevertheless, the rebellion had been seen as a great threat to the big estates and the way of life of those who owned them, and their yeomen had cracked down on the rebels with the greatest severity. Joshua wondered where Captain Dickey had served during the rebellion, and if it was true that some yeomen had hanged rebel leaders on the spot. In any event, he knew that if ever Captain Dickey caught up with Thomas Archer, he for one would be shown no mercy. Being a deserter as well as a rebel, he could expect no quarter from the military.

'Now, Mr Watson,' said Colonel Clavering, 'What can I do for you?'

'Your men have arrested one of my tenants, a weaver by the name of Nathaniel Johnston.'

'And his son, Samuel,' added Joshua.

'So they have,' said the colonel. He took up a report from his desk and leafed through it. 'This weaver should have stayed at his loom. He was out on the streets with the rest of the rabble when you and Mr Davison and the yeomen cavalry were fighting for your lives in the Market House.'

'He was forced to join them,' replied Mr Johnston.

'He's no more a United Irishman than I am.'

Colonel Clavering got to his feet and looked out through the window, his hands again clasped behind his back. 'Then why did Thomas Archer and the so-called Dr Linn call to his cabin?'

So, somebody else had seen the United leaders leaving Sammy's house, Joshua thought.

'I told you,' said Mr Watson, 'they wanted to know why he wasn't in the movement. They forced him to join.'

'They threatened to hazel-whip him – or worse,' added Joshua.

'Worse?' asked the colonel.

Joshua nodded. 'They told him that if he didn't join them the moiley monster would make them pay.'

Colonel Clavering looked at Captain Dickey, who explained, 'It's a local saying. When the United Irishmen kill an informer, the word spreads that he's been devoured by a cow called a moiley.'

Not being an Irishman, Colonel Clavering was clearly perplexed by this explanation, but before he could question it further, Mr Watson said 'They threatened to kill him. Anyway, the point is, I wouldn't be alive today if it wasn't for him. When I escaped from the Market House, he came looking for me. I was wounded, and he succeeded, at great risk to himself, in getting me out to the safety of the Moravian settlement at Gracehill.'

Colonel Clavering nodded and, as if remembering an oversight, asked, 'And how is your arm?'

'It's all right now – but it wouldn't have been if Nathaniel hadn't found me first.'

'And if it hadn't been for Sammy,' said Joshua, 'we'd have been in trouble too.'

'We?' asked the colonel.

'Me, and Naomi, my little sister. We were hiding in the loft above the stables. Sammy took us down to his house, and his mother hid us until Mr Johnston came and took us all out to Gracehill.'

'Very well,' said the colonel, and nodded to Captain Dickey, saying, 'You can let them go.'

'You're also holding two other people,' continued Mr Watson. 'Two people of no real consequence – Timmy Corr and Matty Meek.'

Captain Dickey whispered something in the colonel's ear and pointed to the list of names.

'They're the town clowns,' explained Mr Watson.

'Nevertheless, they were parading with the United men,' said Colonel Clavering. 'And one of them, what's his name ...?' Captain Dickey pointed to the list again. 'Ah yes, Matty Meek, he had a musket.'

Mr Watson smiled and, indicating with his hand, said, 'Sure he's only this height.'

'And everybody knows the musket had no flintlock,' said Joshua.

'It was as much use as the broom Timmy Corr had,' said Mr Watson. 'They were only acting the eejit.'

'But they were parading with the United Irishmen,' insisted Captain Dickey.

'Before the rebellion, I saw them marching behind the Antrim Militia,' recalled Joshua. 'It's all the same to them. They don't know the difference.'

Colonel Clavering sighed, and with a wave of his hand told Captain Dickey, 'All right, let them out. Now, Mr Watson, is there anything else?'

Mr Watson took a deep breath. 'As a matter of fact there is. You're holding two men by the name of Montgomery, an uncle and nephew.'

'Ah, the Montgomerys.' Colonel Clavering, who was sitting on the side of the desk again, nodded, 'We are indeed.'

'The uncle's a farmer, the nephew a carpenter,' explained Mr Watson. 'Both hardworking people, I'm told.'

'Then they shouldn't have swapped the ploughshare for the sword,' said the colonel.

'But what have they done?' asked Mr Watson.

The colonel got up and looked out through the window again. 'One of your most revered magistrates lies gravely ill, knocked to the ground and most severely abused, when his only crime was to try and talk sense to these people. The Montgomerys not only took part in that attack, they openly boasted about it.'

'What are you going to do with them?' asked Joshua, mindful of the dreadful punishment he had seen being meted out in the flogging field.

'They'll get a fair trial,' answered Colonel Clavering. 'Then they'll hang. Furthermore, the people of this town will have the opportunity to demonstrate their loyalty.'

'I thought we had already done that,' protested Mr Watson.

'Some of you,' the colonel told him, 'but not all.'

'Just one other thing,' said Mr Watson, 'If I may. We, the townspeople that is, feel very badly about the billeting of your troops in our places of worship. The seats have been broken up and used as firewood. It's sacrilege.'

Colonel Clavering walked over to the door in a way that clearly indicated the meeting was at an end. 'What happened in this town was sacrilege,' he replied, 'And the people who live here must bear some of the responsibility for it.'

10

Paying the Price

In the rolling hills above the River Main, a lark fluttered up from the grass and eased itself into the bright blue sky. Its song was sweet and crystal clear. Rising and falling in the warm summer air, it carried far across the countryside and tumbled like notes of music on those who laboured on the peat bogs of Kildowney.

'I wonder,' said Sammy, 'what they would have done with us.'

'Probably flogged you,' Joshua replied. 'Maybe even hanged you.'

'What for?'

'I dunno. "Compassing and imagining the death of the king," most likely.'

Sods of peat that were being cut for fuel were being laid out to dry, while others, harvested on previous occasions, had been built into stacks to await collection. As the boys lay with their back against one of these stacks, they could feel the heat of the sun on their bare arms and feet. From somewhere high in the sky came the song of the lark again and, looking up, Sammy found himself squinting into the sun. Pulling his hat down to shade his eyes, he asked, 'What do you mean, "imagining the death of the king?" '

Joshua shrugged. 'I read it in the paper – some man was charged with compassing and imagining the death of the king. It was really treason they were talking about, but that's what it said.'

'And how could they accuse us of that?'

'Well, if they thought you were conspiring with Archer and his friends, they could accuse you of anything they liked.'

'It's just as well you and your father were able to speak up for us,' said Sammy. The song of the lark drifted across the bog again, and he added, 'What was it like? Over at the flogging field?'

'I wouldn't wish it on my worst enemy,' Joshua told him. 'I mean, five hundred lashes! And some of them weren't much older than we are. By the time it was finished, they were just a mess. If it hadn't been for the blood you could have seen their bones.'

'I wonder what they did to deserve that?'

Joshua shook his head. 'Dear knows. But it's nothing to what they're going to do to the Montgomerys.'

'Do you think they really will hang them?' asked Sammy.

'Someone will – the question is, who?' Before Joshua could continue, his Uncle Matthew, who was sitting on the heather with Moses, got up and came over to them.

'I want you to get more buttermilk,' he told them. 'This is thirsty work, and we've run out.'

Sammy, who hadn't met Matthew before, could see that he was short and stout and dressed in a manner befitting his role as part-owner of the bog. Whereas the men who worked for him had rounded hats with curled-up brims and toiled in shirt-sleeves and bare feet, he wore a black three-cornered hat, a black swallow-tailed coat with matching waistcoat, black breeches and black shoes. The coat and waistcoat were stained and obviously far from his Sunday best, yet the attire marked him out as a person of some standing in the district.

'Take that jug,' he told them. 'Better still, take the two of them, and go up to Mr Love's house. If he's not in, one of his sisters will fill them up for you. Tell them I'll pay them later.'

'Can I come too?' cried Naomi, who had been playing with some other children nearby.

'I don't know,' said Joshua. 'It's a long walk.'

'Uncle Matthew, please, can I go too?'

Matthew nodded. 'All right, but stay with Joshua.'

'And don't go wandering off on your own,' warned

Moses. 'I promised your mother I'd keep an eye on you.'

Matthew sat down beside Moses again. 'They can help you to load the cart when they come back.'

Moses smiled. 'That's the easy part of it.'

Matthew agreed. 'Aye, the cutting's the hard part. But then, I've plenty of help.'

Moses looked at the men and women who had been doing the cutting and were now sitting here and there among the heather, taking a break. 'It seems to me you've more than enough.'

'Aye,' said Matthew, and nodding towards a distant road added, 'And there's your reason.'

Moses could just make out a column of red-coated soldiers marching down the road.

'After the rebellion they all want to show they're ordinary, hard-working people.' Matthew continued.

'Do you think they were involved?' asked Moses.

'I would be surprised if they weren't,' said Matthew.

'Did the rebels give you any trouble?'

'No, mind you,' said Matthew. 'Some of them did call on the way into the town, but it was usually only a bite to eat or a drink of water they wanted.' He took out his short clay pipe and lit it. 'Before all this trouble, of course, we had a call from Mr Archer and his men. We all had, every house in this district.'

'What did they want?' asked Moses.

'Oh, the usual – guns, powder, any weapons they could lay their hands on. All I had was my pistol, but they didn't find it. I just told them they were welcome to anything they wanted, and that seemed to satisfy them. They didn't look very hard, but the Loves weren't having any of it. James saw them off in double-quick time.'

Moses grunted and smiled, 'Aye, he always was a tough old coot, just like his father. Is the father still alive?'

'In truth he is,' said Matthew. 'Still living there with James and the two daughters. But, tell me, what's all this I hear about the Montgomerys? Is it true Colonel Clavering

has told the people of the town they must provide a hangman?'

Moses nodded. 'Either that or they'll have to pay a fine
of fifty pounds.'

'And where would they get money like that?' wondered
Matthew.

'There's a reward out for information leading to the
capture of Archer and his gang,' Moses told him. 'Maybe
he's hoping some of them will collect that.'

Matthew shook his head. 'Who would have thought
things would have come to such a sorry pass. And what
about the magistrate? I heard he had died from his
wounds.'

'To tell you the truth, I don't know,' said Moses. 'The
last I heard he was supposed to be on the mend. Which
reminds me: I take it you know Lord O'Neill died from
the wounds he received up in Antrim?'

As the two men talked, the figures of the three who had
gone for the buttermilk receded down the cart track.

'He doesn't look much like your father,' remarked
Sammy.

'Who, Uncle Matthew? Sure he's my mother's brother,
not his,' said Joshua. 'This is where my mother was born,
you know.'

'What's Mr Love's house like?'

'That's it up there on the hill, just across from Uncle
Matthew's.'

'But what's it like inside?' asked Sammy.

'It's lovely,' Joshua told him. 'It's got an upstairs and
everything. They've their own carriage too. Mr Love and
his sisters go to church in it every Sunday. His father's old.
He stays at home.'

'I'm tired, Joshua,' moaned Naomi. 'Can I have a
piggy-back?'

'I told you it was too far for you,' said Joshua. However,
he hunkered down so that she could climb up on to his
shoulders, and a short time later they arrived at Mr.

Love's back yard.

On opening the gate, they saw an elderly man sitting on a stool outside the door. His back was to them, and Sammy asked, 'What's he doing?'

'That's Mr Love's father,' whispered Joshua. 'He's always plaiting straw.'

Sammy could see that the old man was sitting on a stool making a straw rope, the beginning of which he had tied to the metal catch on the doorpost. 'What's it for?' he asked.

'They call it *sugán* harness. It's for pulling the plough. Mr Love says it's strong and cheap. Everybody uses it in the country. It's well seen you're from the town.'

Sammy couldn't imagine a horse pulling a heavy wooden plough with plaited straw. 'I bet it's not as strong as linen,' he said.

Suddenly the old man dropped everything and hobbled into the house as fast as he could, closing the door behind him.

Puzzled, Joshua let Naomi slide off his back and, taking her by the hand, went over to the door and knocked. There was no reply. 'That's strange,' he said. 'I wonder what frightened him?'

There was a creaking noise from up the yard, and turning they saw the barrel of a small pistol appearing round the open doorway of the carriage shed. Joshua picked Naomi up in his arms and was about to tell Sammy to run for it, when a bald, portly man came out of the shed.

With a sigh of relief, Joshua put Naomi down again, saying, 'It's all right. It's only Mr Love.'

'Ah, it's you, Joshua,' called Mr Love. He dropped the pistol into the pocket of his coat and, reaching back around the doorway of the shed, took out a silver-handled cane. He then adjusted his coat, though it must have been many years since one had met across the vast expanse of his stomach and, with his composure regained, came over to meet them. 'Sorry if I frightened you,' he said, 'but you can't be too careful these days.'

'We came over from the bog to get some buttermilk,' Joshua told him. 'Uncle Matthew sent us. This is my friend Sammy.'

Mr Love smiled, and having shaken hands with Sammy said, 'Now this must be, let me see ... Naomi, isn't it? My, but you're getting a big girl.'

Naomi smiled, delighted that someone should think she was getting big, and Joshua added, 'It was Sammy's family that got us all out to Gracehill safely, after the battle for the Market House.'

'Was it indeed?' wheezed Mr Love. 'Lucky for you it was them that found you, and not that scoundrel Archer.' He knocked on the door with the handle of his cane, first three times, then twice more. Slowly the door opened, and they were allowed inside.

Mr Love's father was sitting in the corner by the open fire. 'Joshua!' he exclaimed. 'I heard someone talking out at the gate. I didn't know it was you.'

'Sorry if we gave you a fright,' Joshua replied. 'This is my friend Sammy. And you know Naomi.'

Mr Love put aside his cane and told his sisters, both of whom were working in the kitchen, to fill up the jugs with buttermilk.

The sisters, who wore bonnets and long dresses, were unmarried. Young people rarely came to the house, and they now proceeded to make a great fuss over their visitors, especially Naomi.

One of them had been lifting and plunging a long spade-like handle into a churn that stood in the middle of the kitchen floor. Bending down to Naomi, she smiled into her face and said, 'Well, as it so happens, I've been churning all morning.' She took the jugs and filled them from a crock of buttermilk which she had left in a cool place, just inside the door. 'Would you like a drink yourselves before you go?'

In the kitchen of the Love farmhouse

'Yes please,' replied Joshua.

'I don't like buttermilk,' said Naomi.

'Buttermilk's no drink for a child,' said the other sister. 'Here, Naomi, come over here and see what I've been baking . . . '

'I was sorry to hear about Master Davison,' said Mr Love. 'I hear he put up a great fight.'

'He did indeed,' said Joshua. 'But he was outnumbered.'

'What did they do with him – I mean, his body? I hope they gave him a decent Christian burial.'

'They took it away in a cart,' said Sammy. 'His and Constable Crawford's, and threw them into a grave up in the churchyard. I think they must have taken the bodies of their own dead back out to their families.'

'It's a pity that ruffian Archer wasn't among them,' said Mr Love. 'He came here looking for guns, you know. But I soon gave him a quick shift.'

Joshua would like to have heard more, but he said, 'We'd better be getting back, Mr Love. It's a long walk. They'll be wondering what kept us.'

Mr Love pushed himself up. 'Tell Matthew to come down and see us when he has a minute.'

Outside the door, Sammy lifted the *sugán* rope and asked, 'Is that really strong enough to pull a plough?'

'It is indeed,' Mr Love told him. 'And it's cheap too. Better than pulling the plough by the horse's tail the way they used to do!' He walked them back out to the gate.

'Thank's very much, Mr Love,' said Joshua. 'Uncle Matthew said he'd pay you later.'

Mr Love gave Naomi an affectionate pat on the head and, looking at Sammy, added, 'Your young friend here's a bit pale. The country air will do him good.'

'Sammy works with his father – he's a weaver,' Joshua explained.

'Well, Sammy,' said Mr Love, 'next time Joshua is coming out to visit his Uncle Matthew, you come with him – and don't forget to come down and see us. We might even be doing some ploughing, and you'll see the *sugán* harness for yourself.'

Sammy promised he would come and they made their way back across the bog. Moses, they found, had already begun to load the cart with sods of peat from one of the stacks. These, they heard Matthew say, had been cut the previous summer and, because of their hardness, would burn longer. They all helped with the loading and when the cart was full they left for the town, Naomi sitting up beside Moses, Joshua and Sammy walking along behind.

The heavy sound of a cannon shot echoed and re-echoed among the hills like a roll of thunder. Those who had gathered in the back room of Mr Watson's inn heard it, and knew it was the evening cannon, fired by the military in their camp three miles away in Broughshane. Somehow it also seemed to underline the ultimatum given to the people of Ballymena by Colonel Clavering – either they pay the fine of fifty pounds or provide a hangman for the Montgomerys.

It was from the hills of Craigbilly, overlooking Broughshane, that the Montgomerys had joined the United Irishmen, and it was to Broughshane that they were taken and tried by a military court.

Having established a garrison in Ballymena, the main body of the military had marched out to Broughshane, where they had set up camp. Their arrival was watched by a number of villagers, mostly women and children, many of those who had been involved in the rebellion having fled. First they had seen the guns of the marching soldiers beaming in the sun, then their red coats. When eventually the soldiers marched in, the villagers saw to their surprise that they were preceded by an unusually large goat. A soldier marched with the mascot in front of the cannon, and the various contingents followed – horsemen of the 22nd Dragoons, regular soldiers of the 64th Regiment, and militiamen from Monaghan, Kerry and Tipperary.

Some of the soldiers were billeted in the houses. The others camped on a nearby hill, and each night, at what was known as the signal hour, a cannon was fired from the camp. What the purpose of this was, the local people did not know, but it reminded them, if any reminder was needed, that the rebellion had failed and the military were now in control.

When the echo of the cannon had died away, those who had gathered in the back room of Mr Watson's inn resumed their discussion. From the darkness nearby, Joshua and his mother listened and wondered what they were going to do.

'What does Colonel Clavering think he's doing?' asked one man.

'Shhush,' said Mr Watson. 'Some of his men are in the rooms upstairs.'

'And that's another thing,' whispered someone else. 'Why should the citizens of this town be put to the expense of providing food and accommodation for his soldiers? It's bad enough that they should take over our churches.'

'The point is,' said the owner of another inn, 'we've been cleaned out by the rebels. Food, drink, everything. That all has to be replaced, and it's going to cost money.'

'More to the point,' said Mr Watson, 'we're innkeepers, not hangmen. And I don't know about any of you, but I couldn't hang a man, no matter what he has done.'

There was silence as he added, 'We've no option. We have to find the money somehow.'

How, or where, they found it, Joshua never discovered. All he knew was that the fine was paid and a date set for the execution.

While the military court had been held in Broughshane, the sentence was that the hanging should take place on top of the Moat at Ballymena, where it could be seen by the townspeople and serve as a warning to anyone else who might still harbour thoughts of rebellion.

However, few ventured out to see it. They remained in their homes, their doors closed, windows darkened, and they spoke only in whispers as they waited for the dreadful procession to arrive in the town.

Even Naomi knew from the subdued voices of her parents that something was wrong. 'I don't like the dark,' she complained.

'Don't worry,' her mother told her, 'it'll be bright soon.'

'I want to go out to play,' she cried after a while.

'Not now,' consoled her mother. 'Not just yet.'

'And why is everybody whispering?' she wanted to know.

Joshua was also upset, not because he couldn't go out, but because he found it difficult to comprehend that someone was about to take away someone else's life, deliberately. It was like the feeling he had experienced the day he had heard the first shots being fired at the Market House, only worse.

'I think I'll go upstairs,' he said.

His parents nodded, and his father added, 'Make sure you stay inside until it's all over.'

'Don't worry,' he said and slipped up to his room.

For a while Joshua lay on his bed, his hands clasped behind his head, staring up at the roof. He couldn't help imagining what the hanging would be like, and it seemed to hold his mind in a trance. Then slowly, very slowly, something seemed to seep into his consciousness and he realized it was the slow but steady tramping of feet. Swinging his legs off the bed, he sat on the edge and listened. The sound was getting louder now, and he knew he hadn't been dreaming.

Leaving his room, he tiptoed down the hall to the window overlooking Mill Street. His mother had drawn the blind, and, almost afraid of what he would see, he pulled back the edge of it. The street was empty, but peering up towards the Market House he glimpsed the colourful tunics of soldiers on horseback. They were moving down into Bridge Street and, realizing that he would see very little from where he was, he hurried back to his room. There he climbed out on to the roof below and lowered himself into the yard. The alleyways were deserted and a few moments later he was in the stables of the inn in Bridge Street. Climbing up to the loft, he crept across the dusty floor to a small opening that served as a window.

Down below, a troop of cavalrymen came into sight. Holding the reins of their prancing horses with one hand, their sabres upright in the other, they took up the entire width of the street. Likewise the foot-soldiers who followed them, their long muskets held upright but at the ready, their bayonets fixed to the barrels. Row after row they came, so that the blades of bayonets seemed as numerous as a crop of corn.

Moving his face to the side of the window to peer further up the street, Joshua saw that the troops were escorting four men in civilian clothes. They were walking behind a horse and cart, and he immediately recognized the two in the middle as the Montgomerys. They were bare-headed, their only clothes being their tattered shirts and breeches. Their hands were tied in front of them with a rope attached to the cart and, as if in a daze, they were tugged along, reluctantly, in their bare feet.

On one side of them was a clergyman with an open Bible in his hands, on the other a man with a coiled rope hanging from one arm. Realizing that this was the hangman the townspeople had been forced to pay for, Joshua drew a sharp breath, but he couldn't take his eyes away from the dreadful procession that filed slowly past beneath the window.

Behind the four came further contingents of foot-soldiers and cavalry and, when the last of them passed, Joshua couldn't help thinking that even Timmy Corr and Matty Meek knew it was a day when they shouldn't mimic the military. Indeed, apart from the four who walked behind the cart, not another civilian was to be seen on the street.

The wait for the news that the hanging and been done seemed even longer than the wait for the procession to arrive. Even then the torment of the townspeople was far from over. Colonel Clavering required one more act of loyalty from them before their lives could return to normal.

'The sentence,' Mr Watson told his wife, 'wasn't only that they should hang, but that their heads should be severed from their bodies and put upon pikes on the Market House.'

Mrs Watson buried her head in her hands, saying, 'Oh, how terrible.'

'Are they really going to cut their heads off?' asked Joshua.

Mr Watson poured himself a glass of brandy and sat down at the table. 'No, *they're* not going to do it.' He put the glass to his mouth and drank the brandy in one gulp. 'We have to do it.'

'What do you mean, we have to do it?' asked his wife, appalled at the very idea.

'We, the townspeople.' Mr Watson poured himself another drink. 'Colonel Clavering says we must do it ourselves – as a demonstration of loyalty – or pay a fine of five hundred pounds.'

'Five hundred pounds!' repeated his wife. 'But where would we get that sort of money?'

Mr Watson shook his head. 'We wouldn't.'

'What are you going to do then?' asked Joshua.

His father finished his glass of brandy, got up and put on his hat. 'All I can do is call a meeting and see what we can work out.'

The meeting was held in another inn that night, and whatever decision was taken was never spoken of again by those who were present. But it was said that with no possibility of raising the money, an agreement was reached that the menfolk of the town should each put his hand to the knife in turn, so that the task should not fall to one in particular. All Joshua knew for certain was that the deed was done. By morning the military had placed the heads of the two Montgomerys on spikes on the ruins of the Market House ... and there they stayed, their hair waving to and fro in the breeze, until they were blackened by flies and the sun.

PART 2

THE OUTLAW

11

Back to God's Acre

Joshua looked up at the lamb and thought it was a strange kind of symbol. It was stepping out as if it was beginning a journey, and it carried a flag across its shoulder with a cross on it. In the circle that enclosed it was a Latin inscription, and he twisted his head to one side in an effort to read it.

'VICIT*AGNUS*NOSTER ... ' he began, knowing that he probably wasn't pronouncing the words properly. 'What does it mean?' he asked.

'It's an ancient Christian symbol that our Church adopted from the very beginning,' said Brother Fridlezius. 'It says, "Our lamb has conquered, let us follow him." '

Suddenly realizing that he was in a place of worship, Joshua whipped off his hat and held it across his chest with what he felt was appropriate reverence. The symbol of the lamb was embroidered on a banner fringed with lace that hung from the pulpit. Continuing to gaze up at it, he asked, 'Is it true Thomas Archer came back here and threatened to shoot your minister?'

Brother Fridlezius sighed. 'It's true all right.'

Joshua turned to face him. 'When?'

'It was Communion Sunday,' Brother Fridlezius told him. 'All the adults of the Place had gathered here for the service when we heard a shot. We subsequently discovered that he had shot through the lock on the door of the warden's house.'

'But isn't that your house?' said Joshua. 'The one next door.'

'Well, it's only mine in as much as it's the warden's house, and I happen to be the warden,' said Brother Fridlezius modestly.

'What did he want?'

'We were all kneeling in prayer when he marched in at the head of his men. He said he wanted arms, but I don't know.' Brother Fridlezius eased himself down into one of the long wooden bench seats, and Joshua sat down beside him. As he recalled the experience, his thin, bony face seemed to become even paler than it usually was. 'Somehow I think he has never forgiven us for what we are – and what we were during the rebellion.'

'How do you mean?' asked Joshua.

'I told you before. We were loyal, but neutral. That's why all were welcome, whatever their religion or politics. I don't think he could accept that. But for whatever reason, he was in a rage when he burst in. As I say, we were kneeling in prayer and when he walked among us we feared he was going to kill us.' Brother Fridlezius paused as he thought of the awful moment. 'We watched him go up to the Communion table where our minister was also kneeling. He put the gun to the minister's head and swore a terrible oath. We felt sure the minister would be killed. All we could do was watch and pray. Thankfully, our prayers were answered. Archer's men must have felt they could not stand in God's house and witness blood being spilt. So they rushed out.'

'What did Archer do then?' asked Joshua.

'He looked at us,' Brother Fridlezius recalled, 'and we looked at him. Then his gun came down and without another word he left too. We stayed where we were until the quietness told us the danger was over. Then we got to our feet, happy to be alive. As you can imagine, there was a heartfelt thanksgiving to our Maker for His wonderful care.'

Joshua looked at the hard clay floor, and thought how fearful the brethren must have felt as they knelt there, not knowing from one moment to the next if they were going to be shot in the back of the head. And he thought how unfair it was. For these people, in what Archer had laughingly called God's acre, had extended a welcome to the families on both sides when they had nowhere else to go.

They got up and walked towards the door. 'The reward posters are calling Archer a brigand,' said Joshua. 'They say he's the head of a gang of dangerous banditti. What do they mean by that?'

'It means,' said Brother Fridlezius, 'that in the eyes of the military he has become a bandit, an outlaw. But they're going to have a job catching him. He seems to be able to come and go as he pleases. Day or night, it makes no difference. And no one who is loyal to the Crown is safe from him.'

They walked through the warden's house to the stone cottage at the back where Brother Fridlezius did his woodcarving.

'Have you finished yet?' Joshua asked him.

'Well, I've finished one of them,' he said, and taking it up from the bench added, 'What do you think?'

Joshua ran his fingers over some of the finely carved leaves. 'It's lovely,' he said.

'There's a ladder lying against the bottom of the shed,' said Brother Fridlezius. 'Bring it around to the front, and we'll put it up.'

Carrying his carving with great care, Brother Fridlezius led the way around to the first door of the church, and waited until Joshua had put the ladder in place. This was the brethren's door, and Joshua wondered, not for the first time, if all the men went into services by one door and all the women by the other. Or was it just the single members who were separated. Holding the ladder steady, he watched Brother Fridlezius climb it with one hand and tack the carving into place above the door. 'At least *your* tree's beginning to spread,' he said.

Realizing that Joshua was referring to a previous conversation about the carving, Brother Fridlezius smiled to himself but didn't look down.

'Captain Dickey has pledged to root out the liberty

tree,' Joshua went on. 'He says he won't rest until he brings Archer and his men to justice.'

Brother Fridlezius came down the ladder and stood back to admire his handiwork. 'Well,' he said, 'he's going to have his work cut out. They seem to be able to do what they want, stirring up rebellion, threatening people. Nobody's safe.' He sat back against a rung of the ladder and leaning his hands on his knees looked Joshua in the eyes. 'Anyway, how come you're not at school?'

Joshua shrugged. 'We still haven't been able to get a new teacher.'

'But that's no reason not to go to school. You must remind your parents that we have good schools here.' When Joshua kicked at the ground and mumbled something he couldn't quite make out, Brother Fridlezius asked, 'Did they get anyone yet for Master Davison's murder?'

Joshua shook his head. 'Just the one. A man from Broughshane called Robert McCleary. He swore he had no hand, act or part in it but they hanged him anyway. I'm sure you heard about it. His head's still up on the Market House with the Montgomerys – or what's left of them.'

Brother Fridlezius nodded and stared at the ground. He knew more than most about the poor wretches who continued to find their way to the gallows on the Moat. More often than not, the military authorities called upon himself or Brother Steinhauer to minister to them on the eve of their execution. He found that whatever they had done, or whatever religion they might be, they were concerned about the salvation of their souls. And sometimes when he would speak to them about repentance and remission of sins, tears would flow down the face of even the most hardened of them.

'There's no doubt,' he said, 'but we live in terrible times.' He stood up and removed the ladder. 'But don't worry. It'll soon be over and then everything will be back to normal. I hope you have noticed that in spite of everything the corn is coming along nicely.'

Joshua nodded. 'It's standing well, and so's the lint.'

Brother Fridlezius took up the ladder and put it across his shoulder. 'We've got a good crop of flax all right. I'll make fine linen. I hope when it comes to harvest time you'll give us a hand.'

'Don't worry, I will.'

'And your friend, Sammy. Tell him I said the fresh air will do him good.'

Joshua promised he would and turned to go.

'And remember what I said about school,' said Brother Fridlezius. 'Tell your parents ...' He looked around and smiled. Joshua had already gone.

The first sure sign that things were getting back to normal came with the return of Jimmy the Post. He was escorted up the town by none other than Timmy Corr and Matty Meek. Marching ahead of him and his horse, they were as proud as peacocks. It was as if nothing had ever happened, the small round figure of Matty, smiling as if he himself was bringing the news, the tall thin figure of Timmy, his head thrown back, hailing everyone he met as Jackie and informing them that Jimmy the Post was back.

Whatever the political affiliation of the townspeople – and there were few now who claimed to have had anything to do with the United Irishman – they were happy to see Jimmy return. Yet it was a subdued sort of welcome, for their curiosity to learn what had happened elsewhere was tempered by a feeling of apprehension as to what the news might be. As a result, they listened quietly to what Jimmy the Post had to say. It was the same when Mr Watson would read from the *News-Letter*. Whatever their thoughts they kept them to themselves, in case their reaction might betray a hidden loyalty. For an unguarded utterance, they knew, might bring upon them the wrath of the military – or of Thomas Archer.

So it was that the people of Ballymena learned how near

the United Irishmen had been to succeeding in County
Antrim, having taken over almost all of it. But they were
an untrained army, a rabble some reports called them, and
after the military had crushed them at the battle of Antrim
town, they had gone on to do the same at Ballynahinch in
County Down. Rebel leaders who hadn't been killed in
battle had been hanged, among them the commander in
the north, Henry Joy McCracken, and the leader in
Down, Henry Munroe. Indeed, many had been the hang-
ings, and of particular interest to Joshua was the news that
the United leader who had killed Constable Crawford had
gone to the gallows in Belfast.

Bit by bit the people also learned about events in the
south, including the death of Lord Edward Fitzgerald from
wounds received during his capture. And they wondered
what he would have thought of the sectarian massacres
that had taken place in parts of Leinster. They learned
how the United army had made a determined stand at
Vinegar Hill in Wexford and how, after defeat there, some
of the rebels had pushed north across the Boyne into
Meath, but had failed to find the support they needed.
What would have happened, they wondered, if the French
had come and given their support to the rebellion? It was a
question that was asked time and again as the menfolk
resumed their meetings in the back room of Mr Watson's
inn. And what would happen if the French came now?
Would the United Irishmen rise again? Would they rally to
Thomas Archer and his men? Or had they had enough?

Down south, it was reported, the rebels who had crossed
the Boyne had been worn down by regular troops and
yeomanry, and the stragglers had made their way back to
the bogs of Kildare. Many fugitives, it was said, were giving
themselves up, availing of an amnesty offered by the new
Viceroy, Lord Cornwallis. However, some were still
refusing to surrender, among them a rebel general in
Wicklow by the name of Joseph Holt. He and his men were
still attacking Government troops, including the militiamen

from Antrim. Like Archer, they were also harrassing people who were loyal to the Crown, especially if they thought they were Orangemen, and doing everything they could to rally former rebels to their cause. To Joshua and his family, and those who discussed such things in the back room, it seemed that Archer and Holt were trying to keep the rebellion going until the French arrived.

July turned to August and the corn crops that had withstood the turmoil of the rebellion turned from green to gold. As Brother Fridlezius had predicted, the long hot summer had produced a bumper harvest. Soon the reaping hooks that had been brandished by the rebels on their march into town would be put to proper use. But first the flax had to be pulled, steeped in dams and spread out to dry. By that time the corn would be ready and it wouldn't wait. If it wasn't cut in time, the ears would fall off and the crop would be lost.

The weather was already changing when the Moravian brethren let it be known that they were looking for local labour to help pull the flax, and it was raining when large numbers of men, women and children responded to the call. As they trooped in from the surrounding countryside, it may have seemed to some that it was always raining when flax was being pulled. A back-breaking job at any time, the wetness added to the general discomfort of grasping the prickly-seeded stems. However, no one complained. Weary of death and destruction, and disillusioned by defeat, they were happy to be back at work, knowing they would be paid in kind and return to their cabins with the food that would keep their families alive.

When the flax had been pulled and tied in bundles with bands of rushes, it was put into dams which the brethren had dug beside a small stream. It was then weighted down with large stones to make sure it was completely covered with water, and morning and evening, for the best part of a fortnight, it had to be trampled to make sure it didn't rise above the surface. This was a job for which Joshua

Harvesting the flax

and Sammy volunteered whenever they could get away. The object, they knew, was to make sure the entire stems were completely rotted so that the outer casing could be scutched off to reveal the linen thread that had grown inside.

It was also great fun hopping from one stone to another in their bare feet, and once when they arrived they found small brown eels curled up on the stones. The rotting flax forced the eels to the surface and when they carried them home in jars they wondered if they were the same as the eels that were caught in Lough Neagh. These were much smaller and, for some reason, they wouldn't stay in the jars. Come next morning, they were gone. During the night, according to Moses, they had slipped out of the jars and headed for the nearest stream. Whether they succeeded, no one ever knew.

Taking Brother Fridlezius at his word, Joshua and Sammy also went to help the brethern to harvest the corn and give the sisters a hand with their camomile. Unlike the flax, the other crops always seemed to be harvested on sunny days, and they found it a welcome break from their work at the inn and the loom. When the crop had been harvested, they would return with a little bit of farm produce by way of pay, and, if they were lucky, a penny in their pocket.

Not surprisingly, Joshua was able to bring his mother some camomile, but what pleased her most was that he also brought home a little knowledge. When they had once again remarked on the fact that the flowers smelled of apples, Sister Hannah had told them that the name camomile came from a Greek word meaning 'earth apple'. Learning a little bit of Greek, the Watsons knew, was something that would also have pleased Master Davison.

Sometimes, when she had a minute to spare, Sister Hannah also showed the young people who came to help in the harvest how to plait cornstraw. Twisting and bending the straw, she would weave it into the most beautiful harvest knots and stars. And when, with a coy smile, she produced one in the shape of a heart, they would all smile and chide her in such a way that she knew they were hoping that some day she would get married. When that happened, they knew, she would exchange the pink ribbon on her white linen bonnet for a blue one.

In the evening, when he returned to the inn, Joshua also showed Naomi how to make harvest knots. Somehow harvesting and the fun that went with it all seemed to make the prospect of a French invasion very unreal. It was only when he heard his parents and others talking that he realized how real the danger still was. Apart from what they had to say about the latest exploits of Thomas Archer, their discussions always seemed to be about the wars France was waging and about reports that fleets of warships had left or were about to leave France.

It wasn't until Jimmy the Post called at the inn one day in late August that they learned the French had landed at Killala in County Mayo. The news was received with alarm at first by those who feared that it would trigger another rebellion, but soon it became apparent that the French had come too late. While many local people joined them, there was no general uprising and, after some spectacular successes, the invaders were defeated. Even Joseph Holt, the rebel leader who was holding out in Wicklow, failed to rekindle the spirit of rebellion, and following the defeat of the French the papers carried reports that the Government was offering Holt terms for surrender.

In Antrim, no such terms were being offered to Thomas Archer or his men. He too had failed to rouse his former comrades-in-arms, but those who knew him were convinced that he would never surrender.

It was a point made by Brother Fridlezius after he had tacked his other woodcarving above the sisters' door of the church. Taking up a quill to update the settlement's diary, he paused for a moment and told Joshua, 'I've looked down the barrel of Archer's pistol. And I've looked into his eyes. There's no way he'll ever give himself up.'

Joshua nodded. He too had looked into the eyes of the outlaw.

Neither knew it then, but the day would come when both would look into the eyes of Thomas Archer again.

12

Rebels and Spies

It was a dark, wet night, and not even those who dared poach rabbits in the Hillhead estate were there to see the black coach that made its way up the winding path to Captain Dickey's mansion. Even if they had been there, it's doubtful if they would have recognised it. Pulled by a single horse, it was a private coach that was sometimes used by the military or their agents, whenever circumstances required that they move around without attracting too much attention. The driver grumbled in the way that soldiers do when they are called out of a warm bed late at night, but if he was a soldier he was in civilian clothes. Taking the reins in one hand, he pulled his greatcoat around him with the other and lowered his head against the driving rain.

Whatever about the coach, no one would have seen, let alone recognized, the man who sat inside, for he was a man who spent his life in the shadows and was seldom seen, except by those who were going to the gallows. Both his hands rested on his walking-cane and occasionally the fingers of one would strum upon the other as he hummed quietly to himself. He listened to the flurries of rain as they pattered on the side of the coach, then to the wind as it whistled through the trees, and was comforted by the thought that the same wind would carry more of the country's troublemakers to the other side of the world.

It was also with some satisfaction that he thought of the fourth head that he had helped to add to the pikes on top of the Market House. John Eggleson, found guilty by court martial of assisting in flogging a man who had died from his wounds, had been taken to the Moat and hanged. Denied it, of course, but then they all did. Another man, also found guilty of assisting in the whipping, had been

Captain Dickey greets his mysterious guest

sentenced to be transported, and ordered to serve the
King of Prussia in the war against France. Ironic, he
thought, that the miscreant should have to fight against
the country that had sided with the United Irishmen.

Instead of drawing up at the front entrance, the coach
went around by the side. When it stopped at a side door
the passenger drew his cloak around him, and holding on
to his black three-cornered hat hurried inside. He had
already left his cane on a side table and hung up his hat
and cloak when Captain Dickey opened the door of his
study and ushered him in. Both the lateness of the hour
and the location of their meeting ensured that no one, not
even family members or servants, would be aware of it.
The only other creature present was the captain's water-
spaniel, and after a wag of the tail which drew no response
from the visitor it curled up on the hearth and went back
to sleep.

As his guest stood with his back to the fire warming
himself, Captain Dickey poured two glasses of brandy,
and handing one to him said, 'Here, that'll warm you up.'

'One thing I'll say for the French,' said the other, noting
the label on the bottle, 'they make damn fine brandy.'

Captain Dickey smiled and pulled up another chair.
'Only a day or two ago I saw in the *News-Letter*, a fellow in
Belfast advertising real French Bordeaux brandy for sale. I
don't know how they manage to get the stuff. But you're
right, they do make fine brandy.'

When they were resting comfortably and suitably warmed by the glow of the fire and the occasional sip of brandy,
Captain Dickey lifted some papers that were lying on a
small table beside him. 'Unfortunately, there are less
palatable things to read about.'

His guest could see that he had lifted a sheaf of cuttings
from the *News-Letter*, but offered no comment.

'It's a full year now since the rebellion,' continued
Captain Dickey, 'and what do we have? Intimidation of
law-abiding citizens.' He took one of the cuttings and,

tilting it towards the light of the fire, read, ' "It is with great concern we mention, that in one or two districts of the county of Antrim some infamous villains continue to bring disgrace on the country by whipping and otherwise maltreating the inhabitants." '

When the other man said nothing, he took up a second cutting and continued, ' "Three persons brought in ... suspected of having been concerned in flogging different persons in this county. Another, called McKellaher, apprehended in the parish of Clough, on suspicion of flogging, safely lodged in Ballymena." '

'Well,' said the other man, 'at least it shows that we are apprehending the culprits.'

'Apprehending culprits, yes,' continued Captain Dickey, 'but hardly the ones we want.' The other man shifted uncomfortably in his chair as he went on, ' "It is hoped that the apprehending of this fellow" – that's McKellaher – "will break up a strong gang, as there are many positive informations against him." But will it? Listen to this: "The following night, a poor man in the parish of Clough was seized by a number of wretches who actually cut off the half of his tongue to prevent his giving information." '

Captain Dickey stood up, and throwing the sheaf of cuttings down on the table told his guest, 'The newspaper editors aren't the only ones that are expressing concern. Dublin Castle wants to know what I – what we – are doing about it. This fellow who had the audacity to try and bring the French in at Lough Swilly – what's his name?'

'Tone,' said the other, 'Wolfe Tone.'

'He died by his own hand last November. And this so-called rebel general down in Wicklow, Joseph Holt – he and his friends have been subdued and are on their way to New South Wales.'

'That's right, and with many hundreds more, I might add.'

'Exactly,' said Captain Dickey, 'and Dublin wants to know what are we doing about Archer and his gang?'

'Don't worry, we'll catch up with them. And when we do, new heads will adorn the Market House.'

'But when, when?' asked Captain Dickey. He sat down and poured two more brandies. 'Perhaps you might talk to a namesake of mine, Mrs Dickey of Kilcreen?'

'Kilcreen?'

Captain Dickey nodded. 'It's eight or nine miles out of town, beyond Kildowney, on the road to Ballymoney. She and her husband William are noted for their loyalty to the Crown ... and that, as you know, is something our friend Archer violently disapproves of.'

'Another flogging? I wasn't aware ... '

'No, not a flogging, and no one is aware of it, except myself, for reasons I will explain to you.'

His guest sipped his brandy and listened.

'Archer paid her a visit, apparently in the belief that she was aware of the whereabouts of his hide-out and might give information to the authorities.'

The other man sat upright again and set his brandy down on the table. 'And does she? I mean, has she?'

'If she does know where his hide-out is, she hasn't told us,' replied Captain Dickey. 'Nor is she likely to, unless we approach the matter with the greatest caution. You see, Archer and his men called at her house in the middle of the night. He levelled a pistol at her head and, according to my information, would have murdered her on the spot, had it not been for the fact that one of his own men pleaded with him not to do so. Naturally, I can't send any of my men into the area to see her, as the sight of a yeoman would suggest that she had contacted the authorities, and then she surely would be murdered.'

'So you think one of my agents should talk to her?'

Captain Dickey reached over and poured him another brandy. 'I do,' he said, and when he had replenished his own glass he added, 'You see, it seems to me, from the incidents that have occurred, that Archer may well have his hide-out in the Kildowney area. Clough, where the poor wretch had his tongue cut off, is only a mile or two up the road.'

The other man nodded. 'You think that was the work of Archer too?'

'I don't really know, but someone was very anxious to prevent him giving information too.'

Having drained his glass the other man got up, and shaking hands with Captain Dickey assured him, 'I'll keep you informed.'

The water-spaniel opened its eyes slightly, as if to show that it had noted his departure, and went back to sleep. It was a sleep in which it may have dreamt of hunting pheasants, but no one, not even Captain Dickey, could have imagined that the spaniel would play a vital part in the hunt for Thomas Archer.

Mrs Watson gathered up three sods of peat and placed them in a triangular shape on the fire. As the flames flickered up around them, she dusted off her long black dress and sat down again. 'When are they going to take those heads down from the Market House,' she asked her husband.

Mr Watson, who was sitting on the other side of the fire, perusing the *News-Letter* by the light of a small lamp, grunted, and resting the paper on his knees told her, 'Whenever the country's back to normal.'

'And when will that be?'

'When they catch this fellow Archer and his friends.'

'Well, the sooner they take those heads down the better,' said Mrs Watson. 'They're a disgusting sight. It's not right that young people like Naomi should have to look at them every time they go out.'

'She doesn't have to look at them,' said Joshua, who was sitting on the other side of the lamp, wrestling with homework his new teacher had given him.

'I do so,' protested Naomi. 'I mean, how can I not look at them? They're awful. Sometimes I feel sick.'

Naomi had grown in the year since the rebellion, and was now going to school with Joshua.

'Matthew called in today,' said Mrs Watson. When Joshua looked up to see if she was addressing him, she continued, 'He says he'll be needing all the help he can get to salvage his crops."

Joshua nodded. If the summer of the rebellion had been warm and sunny, the present one had turned out to be the opposite. There had been snow in April and now the rain was raising fears for the harvest. Little wonder Matthew was letting it be known that he would be needing help.

'Maybe you and Sammy could go out and give him a hand,' his mother went on.

'Sure his father needs him to help with the weaving,' said Joshua.

'I know he does,' said Mrs Watson. 'But as it so happens I've been talking to his mother. She's worried about him.'

Joshua looked up. 'Why, what's wrong with him?'

'She says he's very pale.'

Mr Watson grunted again to indicate that while he was reading the paper he was listening to her, and added, 'He's always pale.'

'The truth is,' said Mrs Watson, 'he needs to get out more. Maybe if you had a word with his father.'

Her husband put the paper down again. 'If you think it will do any good. But the truth is Nathaniel needs all the help he can get.'

'The truth is,' said Mrs Watson, 'Matthew will be needing all the help *he* can get, and the fresh air will do Sammy good.'

'Mr Love said the very same thing last year,' Joshua told them, 'when we went up to his house to get buttermilk. He said what Sammy needed was to get out in the air. He said the next time I was going to see Uncle Matthew I should bring him along. And he wants us to call and see him. He said he'd show us how to make *sugán* harness.'

'Is the old man still at that?' mused his father. 'Well, I suppose it keeps him occupied.'

'Why don't you have a chat with Nathaniel?' urged Mrs Watson, determined not to let the matter pass.

'That's a great idea,' exclaimed Joshua.

Ignoring Joshua's enthusiasm, his father asked, 'And who would help him with the weaving?'

Mrs Watson dusted an imaginary fleck of turf mould from her dress in a gesture that was meant to lend authority to her reply. 'We'll come to some arrangement. Anyway, if he helps Matthew, I'm sure he won't come home empty-handed. And, as I said, it'll do him good.'

As it turned out, Matthew was among the lucky ones. With the help of Sammy and Joshua and a host of others, he managed to save a portion of his flax and some of his corn. The rest was beaten down by the rain, the grass grew up through it and it rotted. In some areas the crops failed completely. Many people were reported to be on the verge of famine and, according to Jimmy the Post, the emigrant ships were full. At the same time the remnants of the rebels were still being shipped out to the penal settlements in New South Wales or to serve in the army of the King of Prussia.

Whatever arrangement his father made with Sammy's father, Joshua never discovered, but when, in late November, Matthew again asked for their assistance, Mr Johnston readily agreed.

Matthew had called at the inn to deliver some badly needed farm produce. Mrs Watson wrapped Joshua up well in a warm greatcoat and found another somewhere for Sammy. As always, their mothers cautioned them to be careful, and off they went. Sitting on the empty cart, they smiled at one another but said nothing. Whatever fear their parents might have for the journey, they knew they were in good hands, for Matthew always carried a small traveller's pistol in the pocket of his greatcoat. Joshua had shown it to Sammy during their last visit to the farm. It had two brass barrels, side by side, and according to the markings on it had been made in London in 1785.

In any event, both of them were delighted to be relieved of duties which, in their own different ways, had become demanding and tedious. All at once they felt free, happy to be heading up the open road and out into the countryside. Normally Naomi would have been crying to go with them, but the memory of the day when they had run into the United Irishmen and the thought of working with cold hands on the farm made her content to wave them goodbye, and rush back to join some of her friends. No one could have guessed that Joshua and Sammy would meet some of the United Irishmen again.

The road to Kildowney had not improved with the rain. Nor had the circumstances of those who lived along the way. The condition of families who came to the doors of dilapidated cabins or crawled out from under other makeshift accommodation to ask for food was heart-rending. Sammy and Joshua had brought some food to eat on the journey, and soon they had given it all away to the little hands that were thrust up to them.

At one stage, Matthew stopped to give a lift to a man and his wife and two young children. They carried all their worldly goods in a bundle, and during the journey they let it be known that they were heading for Londonderry, in the hope of getting on board an emigrant ship. How they hoped to pay for their passage wasn't clear, but before they parted Matthew reached into his waistcoat pocket and slipped the man a coin. Joshua hoped it was a guinea, but he had no way of knowing. The man thanked Matthew profusely and the family continued on a journey that could lead to anywhere.

'I hope they won't be robbed,' said Sammy, as they watched them go.

Joshua nodded. 'I hope not.' He also hoped that nothing else would befall them, and that they wouldn't end up on one of the other ships he had heard about – the ones that took people to Van Diemen's Land or Botany Bay.

Matthew's wife, May, was delighted to see them. No sooner had they come in than she had their coats off and was making them warm themselves at the open fire. Sammy knew from his previous visit that it was a fire she never allowed to go out. Joshua and he had slept up in the loft opposite the fire, and he had seen her, early in the mornings, leaning down to blow on the white ash of the peat to make it glow again.

Matthew and May had no children, and that, Sammy reckoned, was part of the reason why they made Joshua and himself so welcome. They had two men who worked around the farm, and occasionally a young woman from the locality came in to give a hand. But by and large May worked every bit as hard as her husband, maybe even harder, for it seemed to Sammy that when there were others around to do the work Matthew considered a supervisory role more in keeping with his standing in the district. Their cottage was much bigger than a weaver's, having a grand total of three rooms. To one side of the kitchen was the bedroom, and above that, opposite the fire, the large open-fronted loft. To the other side of the kitchen was a parlour, but that was something Sammy had only seen once, when Joshua had let him peep in. At one end of the cottage was a substantial stack of peat, at the other a cowbyre, which they would be required to muck out.

When they had warmed themselves, Joshua and Sammy sat on the long wooden bench-seat beside the dresser and leaned their arms on the table, while May got them something to eat. The bench, they knew, opened up into what was called a settle bed, but they had never seen it opened. The kitchen was the central part of the cottage, the part that kept everything else going. The floor, Sammy noted, had flagstones, unlike the clay floor in his own home. There was a griddle over the peat fire, another smaller table with crocks of buttermilk under the window, and a

wooden dash-churn, with its long-handled plunger, standing nearby. According to Joshua, the young woman
who came in to help did much of the plunging or dashing
that was required for the churning. Otherwise May tied
back her long greying hair and did the rest. Her black
dress was shorter than those of the women in the town,
and Sammy had also observed that when she was out in
the yard looking for duck eggs, she wasn't averse to
hitching it up, in the way that country women do, to step
over a fence.

Over the next few days they helped with various jobs
around the farm. Sometimes, when Matthew didn't need
them, they would explore the woods and scrubland up at
the back, or go down to Mr Love's farm to see how the
old man plaited the *sugán* ropes. When darkness came,
and everything was locked in for the night, they would sit
on the warm flagstones in front of the fire and listen to the
talk. It was the custom of some of the neighbouring men
to call in, and when they were all seated around the fire,
puffing at their short clay pipes, they would discuss the
problems of farming and the weather. As one thing led to
another, they would also tell stories. Some of these would
be ghost stories, but, more often than not, they would end
up talking about Thomas Archer and the other outlaws
who continued to cause trouble in the area.

The newspaper was even slower coming to country
areas than to the town, and when Matthew received a
copy it was always a good few days old. Nevertheless it
proved of great interest, not only to him and his wife, but
to the neighbours. While May would hold the candle over,
so that he could see better, he would pick out interesting
bits and read them aloud. Like the report he read out one
night of a court martial in Belfast. The military court had
sentenced a woman to three months in solitary
confinement for gross prevarication. For one month of
that time she was to be fed on bread and water only.

'Bread and water,' said one of the men. 'Boys a boys.'

'And all for prevar ... prevar ... ' said another.

Before he could finish, Joshua asked, 'What is prevarication anyway?'

His Aunt May smiled. 'I think it means she wouldn't answer their questions.'

'Aye,' said the other men and they nodded and sucked their clay pipes with satisfaction, now that they knew what it meant. 'Prevarication.'

Matthew also read to them a report that a man had been inhumanly murdered, and other country people wounded, by a sergeant in the Templepatrick yeomanry, adding, 'A considerable reward is offered for the apprehension of this miscreant.'

'A sergeant in the yeomanry,' said one of the neighbours. 'Imagine that.'

Turning to Joshua, Matthew asked, 'Have you still got the yeoman's button that you found on Master Davison's body?'

Joshua nodded, and taking it out of his breeches' pocket, handed it around for the others to see. They had all seen it before, of course, but that didn't keep them from turning it over and examining it again with great curiosity.

'D/C,' commented one of them.

Another nodded, and taking the button, added, 'Dunseverick Cavalry.'

'I keep it as a lucky piece,' explained Joshua.

The men grunted by way of understanding, and one said, 'I wonder what came over the yeoman sergeant in Templepatrick?'

'Must have been recruited by the United Irishmen,' said Matthew.

'And you say there's a reward for him?' the neighbour went on.

'How much do you think is on the head of Thomas Archer now?' asked another.

'Must be a hundred guineas,' said Matthew. 'Maybe more.'

'Aye, could be two or three hundred,' someone else said. 'Not to mention the rewards that are being offered for Dr Linn, Roddy McCorley and the others.'

'It's a wonder nobody has tried to collect it,' put in Sammy. 'Especially with times being so hard as they are.'

'No one would dare tell the military where they were,' said one of the men, 'even if they did know.'

'And you can't tell if you haven't a tongue in your head,' said another.

'Or if you're dead,' said somebody else.

'What do you mean, if you haven't a tongue in your head?' asked Joshua.

'They cut off a man's tongue up at Clough,' said the man who had made the remark. 'They must have been afraid he was going to talk.'

'You mean Archer and his men?' asked Sammy.

The man shook his head. 'No one knows who did it.'

Matthew reached into the fire for a light and lit up his pipe again. 'They say,' he began, expelling a lungful of smoke and coughing in the process. 'They say Archer threatened Mrs Dickey over at Kilcreen.'

'What for?' asked Sammy.

'I don't rightly know,' Matthew told him. 'Nobody does.'

'She must have found out something about him,' said one of the visitors. 'But whatever it was, you can be sure she's not going to tell anybody now.'

'Not if she values her life,' said another.

'I heard,' said May, taking care not to mention who had told her, 'that he put a pistol to her head and was going to shoot her, but one of his own men persuaded him not to.'

Joshua and Sammy listened as they talked late into the night, and later, when the neighbours had gone, they climbed up into the loft and snuggled into the bedclothes. The white walls were bathed in the warm comforting glow of the fire, and for a while they lay looking up at the white ends of the hazel sticks that held the thatch in place.

Neither spoke, but they were thinking about some of the things that had been said. Somewhere out there, they knew, were Thomas Archer and his gang of outlaws. A short time later, they were relieved to hear Matthew closing both parts of the door and pushing home the bolts to make them secure. Gradually the glow of the peat fire died down, darkness crept up around them, and they went to sleep.

For both of them it was a restless sleep, a sleep disturbed by dreams of leering faces and long flashing knives that threatened to cut out their tongues. Several times they awoke with a start, and when, at long last, morning came, they vowed that if ever they came across the outlaws again their lips would be sealed. There was no way they were going to tell anyone, even their parents. Whatever about their fear of the moiley cow, they were not going to risk ending up like the man from Clough.

It was a vow that would soon be put to the test. For even as they awoke, Thomas Archer and his men were riding towards Kildowney.

13

Ali Baba

It was only when a blackbird came screeching up a hedge-row that Joshua and Sammy realized something was wrong.

Like most cottages, Matthew's had two sources of water. One was rain-water, which was collected in a barrel under the thatch and used for washing. The other was spring water, which was kept in a wooden bucket on a stool beside the table. It was for drinking. Whenever the drinking water got low, the remainder was poured into one of the heavy black pots that hung over the fire, and someone, usually May herself, made the long journey down the hill to the spring. Having dipped the bucket she would then begin the somewhat arduous climb back to the house. With two to carry the bucket, the task became much easier, and her two young visitors were happy to do it for her. Sometimes they would collect watercress from the muddy stream that flowed away from the spring, and when they had eaten it they would slake their thirst by lying down and drinking directly from the small pool of crystal clear water.

Blackbirds, they knew, were forever raising an alarm about something, especially towards dusk. This one had come screeching up the hedgerow from Mr Love's farm, and now, as it balanced itself on a hawthorn tree a short distance from the spring, it continued to sound a warning 'pink, pink, pink'.

'Probably a stoat,' said Joshua.

'Or a fox,' added Sammy.

Joshua nodded, and was about to dip the bucket into the spring when a pistol-shot rang out. 'Where did that come from?' he asked, scrambling to his feet.

'Sounded as if it was down at Mr Love's.'

Leaving the bucket on the grass, they sprinted down towards the farm, and a few moments later were at the back yard.

'I wonder what's going on?' asked Sammy breathlessly.

They could hear the sound of raised voices now and, realizing that something was wrong, they made their way up between the farm buildings until they were at a small stone outhouse that held some pigs.

Taking off his hat, Joshua peeped around the corner. 'There's a group of men around the door of the house,' he gasped, 'and one of them's holding a gun to the old man's head.'

Sammy got down on one knee, and peering around the corner said, 'It's Archer. Look, that's the blunderbuss he's pointing at him.'

'You're right, it *is* him,' whispered Joshua. 'Listen! What are they saying?'

'They're talking to the people in the house,' said Sammy. 'They're saying they'll shoot the old man if they don't open the door and let them in.'

The pigs in the shed began to squeal and they pulled back their heads, in case the men might look down and see them.

Joshua put his hat back on his head. 'We'd better tell Uncle Matthew.'

'Right,' panted Sammy. 'Come on.'

All thoughts of the bucket of water forgotten, they ran back up through the fields, taking care to keep to the cover of the hedges in case they might be seen. Matthew and two of his men were in an outhouse, sorting out some potatoes, when they ran in and blurted out the news.

'Wait here,' said Matthew, and running over to the cottage, reappeared a few moments later with his pistol. Pausing only long enough to pour in the powder that would fire it, he put the powder-flask into his pocket and hurried down the fields. Joshua and Sammy and the two workmen followed at a discreet distance.

'Be careful,' called May as loudly as she dared, but if they heard they didn't turn around. Their eyes were focussed on Mr Love's farmhouse, wondering what was going on, yet afraid of drawing the attention of the outlaws upon themselves by going too close too soon.

They had ventured down as far as the spring well when another shot rang out from the direction of the farmhouse. It was a louder, heavier shot this time, and the boys reckoned it was the sound of Archer's blunderbuss. The shot was followed by loud screams. There was a lot of shouting. Then the sound of galloping horses.

Matthew had now reached the outhouses, and seeing him running up towards Mr Love's farmhouse the others followed. By the time they reached the farmhouse door Matthew had come back out again. He was in a state of considerable agitation. 'Don't go in there,' he told them.

'Why? What's happened?' asked Joshua.

Matthew lowered his pistol and, as they waited for his reply, they noted that a partly finished *sugán* rope hung limply from the catch on the door post 'They've killed Mr Love,' he told them. Almost before they could comprehend the dreadful news, he bade them, 'Go up to the house and tell May to come down. The sisters are in a bad way. So's the old man.'

Joshua and Sammy needed no second bidding. Holding on to their hats, they took off across the yard as fast as they could.

'And stay there,' Matthew called after them. 'I'll be up as soon as I can.'

May had reached the spring well and was waiting anxiously to hear what was going on. Even before the boys came up to her she realized something dreadful had happened, and holding up the hem of her black dress she hurried down to the house to give what solace she could.

When Matthew came back up to his own house, he saddled one of his horses. It was almost dark now and, telling the boys to go inside and bolt the doors, he rode off to alert the military.

In the days that followed, red-coated soldiers, long bayonets fixed to the ends of their muskets, could be seen combing the woods and bogs of the area. Occasionally a shot was heard, raising the expectation of news that the outlaws had been captured. However, no such news arrived. Whenever a troop of cavalry galloped up into the yard, it was usually to look for directions or a drink of water. Once again, it seemed, Thomas Archer had got away.

The killing of Mr Love changed everything. Apart from the grief caused by the loss of such a good friend and neighbour, Matthew and May now lived in fear that they might be next on Archer's list. May didn't venture out of doors unless she had to and, even when going about his daily chores on the farm, Matthew carried his pistol. The top half of the door, which had always been open during the day, was now closed and bolted whenever anyone was inside, and wasn't opened until those outside were identified. When darkness came, Matthew took the added precaution of standing to one side of the door with his pistol at the ready, in case the caller might not be welcome.

'If only we knew why they killed him,' said May.

It was several nights after the murder, and they were sitting at the fire, talking it over for the umpteenth time. No neighbours had come and no one was surprised. It went without saying that the men who usually called were required in their own homes. They, no doubt, were also sitting behind closed doors trying to make sense of what appeared to be a senseless killing.

'We all know why they killed him,' Matthew asserted. His clay pipe lay on the hob; somehow, it seemed, he didn't have the heart to smoke it. 'It was because he was loyal to the Crown.'

There was silence for a moment, then Joshua told them, 'The day we were here for the load of peat. Remember, we came with Moses? We saw Mr Love with a pistol.'

'That's right,' said Sammy. 'We walked across the bog to his house, to get you some buttermilk.'

'What was he doing with it?' asked Matthew.

'When we walked into the yard he pointed it round the door of the carriage shed,' Joshua recalled.

'He put it away when he saw it was only us,' said Sammy.

'He was saying he had some run-in with Archer,' Joshua went on.

'That's right,' said Sammy. 'He said he gave Archer a quick shift when he came looking for guns. Do you think maybe that's why Archer killed him.'

'It could be, all right,' Matthew replied, 'but somehow I doubt it. That was nearly two years ago and he hasn't bothered him since.'

'Matthew and I were wondering,' said May. She was speaking slowly, choosing her words carefully. 'Would they have seen you, by any chance, when you ran down into the yard?'

Joshua looked at Sammy, then shook his head. 'I don't think so. Why?'

'Well, if they did,' said Matthew, 'you could be in some danger.'

'I don't see how,' said Sammy. 'I mean, his sisters saw them too. And his father. They all know who it was.'

May got up and put several more sods of peat on the fire. 'That's right,' she said. 'They did see them. But maybe Archer reckons they'll be too afraid to talk.'

'If he thought you two could identify him,' Matthew explained, 'it would be a different matter.'

'You mean, he might come after us?' asked Joshua.

'It depends on whether they saw you or not,' said Matthew.

Joshua took a deep breath and expelled it slowly. 'So what do you think we should do?'

'I think you should both head back into the town first

thing in the morning.'

'Just to be on the safe side,' added his wife.

Joshua hesitated. 'We wouldn't want to be leaving you in any danger.'

May smiled. 'We'll be all right. But we'd feel happier if the two of you were back home safely.'

'You can take the horse and cart,' said Matthew.

'Will you be going with us?' asked Joshua.

Matthew shook his head. 'I think I'd better stick around here. You can take some potatoes in with you, and I'll collect the cart later, after this trouble blows over.'

'And when it does,' said May, 'I hope you'll come out to see us again.'

Joshua and Sammy promised they would. Matthew checked the door to make doubly sure it was bolted, and they all turned in.

For a long time, Joshua and Sammy lay awake, thinking about what had been said and occasionally talking about it. It hadn't occurred to them that they themselves might be in danger now. But the more they thought about it, the more they reckoned Matthew and May were right. As a result, they found it difficult to get to sleep. Whenever they dozed, a noise outside would jolt them back to life and they would lie wondering if someone was prowling around, perhaps trying to find a way in. After a while they would come to the conclusion that it must have been a cat or a dog or maybe only the wind ... Even so, they had a great sense of unease and longed for the night to pass.

Just when they went to sleep they couldn't remember, but suddenly it was morning. May was blowing the ashes back to life in the open fire below them, and Matthew, they could see, was getting ready to go out.

By the time they had eaten their breakfast and put on their greatcoats, Matthew and one of his men had yoked the horse up to the flat cart. The cribs, or sides, had been put on the cart and some potatoes and other vegetables heaped in the back.

Covering the produce with straw, Matthew told Joshua, 'Give these to your mother and father.' He smiled, and ruffling Sammy's mousy hair, added, 'Tell them some of them are for Sammy's folks.'

'Don't worry, I will,' said Joshua.

'Thanks very much for everything,' said Sammy.

'You earned your keep,' Matthew replied. 'And a bit more.' Reaching into his pocket, he dropped several coins into the hand of one, then the other. Before they could thank him properly, he had given them a leg up into the cart, and handed the reins to Joshua. 'Now, keep going,' he warned them. 'And don't stop for anybody, be he beggarman or thief.'

They waved to May, who had also brushed aside any word of thanks for her hospitality, and, with Matthew's warning words ringing in their ears, they were soon heading back down the road to Ballymena.

Everything went well until the boys reached a spot beyond the bog where the narrow road twisted and turned between high hedges. Without warning, two men jumped out in front of them. One grabbed the horse by the halter, while the other jumped up into the cart and, pointing a pistol at their backs, ordered them to turn up a narrow track to their right.

'We haven't anything worth stealing,' Joshua protested. 'Look!' He put his left hand in his pocket to show it was empty, but then remembered the money his Uncle Matthew had given him.

'It's not your money we want,' said the man with the pistol. 'Now keep going.'

The second man had climbed aboard now, and Joshua gave a flick of the reins to get going again. Sammy's face, he could see, was pale, paler than ever, and he knew his friend was thinking the same as he was. If these men weren't highwaymen, they must be United Irishmen. And, if they didn't want their money, it was them they wanted.

Suddenly the words of Matthew and May came flooding back into his mind. 'Would they have seen you by any chance?' 'If they did, you could be in danger.'

'Keep going,' Matthew had warned, 'and don't stop for anybody, be he beggarman or thief.' But now they had been stopped, a pistol was pointing at their backs, and they were being carried further and further away from the main road.

Even as these thoughts raced through Joshua's mind, another one added to his terror, and he was glad the men hadn't grabbed the few pence that his uncle had given him. For when he had reached into his pocket, his fingers had found, not only the coins, but the button that had fallen from Master Davison's pocket. 'D/C' it said, and the United Irishmen would know well what that meant. He knew how they hated the yeomen cavalry, especially after the way the yeomen had hanged some of their leaders during the rebellion.

Taking the reins in one hand, he reached into the pocket of his breeches with the other and, locating the button, extracted it with finger and thumb. He was tempted to drop it on to the ground, but it was his lucky piece and, anyway, the men might see it falling or hear it bouncing off the front of the cart. Below the left pocket of his greatcoat, he knew, was a triangular tear where he had caught it on a sharp edge while working on his uncle's farm. Without looking, he moved his hand down until he found the tear and pushed the button inside with his thumb. Later, if he was lucky, he could retrieve it.

Out of the corner of his eye, Sammy could see what Joshua was doing, and, in an effort to attract the men's attention away from him, asked, 'Where are you taking us? What do you want?'

The man with the pistol pushed the barrel between them so that they could see it and replied, 'Just keep going. You'll find out soon enough.'

For what seemed hours they wound their way through

In rebel hands

narrow lanes and tracks. Joshua and Sammy kept their eyes skinned for any sign of scarlet that would indicate the military were in the area, but there was none. They hoped against hope that around every bend they would come upon a group of soldiers, but it was not to be. After what seemed an eternity, the two men made them sit down in the back of the cart and put blindfolds on them. Another long, bumpy journey followed, and they reckoned it must have been late afternoon when the cart finally came to a halt.

Blinking to adjust their eyes to the light, they could see they had arrived at a thatched cabin. It was small and dirty. The thatch had rotted here and there, and the lime that had once whitened it was flaked and damp. The area all around it was overgrown with trees and scrub, hiding it completely from the outside world, and they wondered where they were.

Somewhere along the way a man with a musket had joined them. Probably a look-out they thought, as they followed the cart around to the back yard. There two men were working at a large wooden barrel, while several others looked on.

'Ah, so you got them,' said one of the men. He was standing with his hands resting on the small of his back, surveying the work. Those words of greeting seemed to confirm their worst fears and then their hearts sank when they saw who it was. It was Thomas Archer. There was no mistaking that short, powerful figure in the green swallow-tailed coat. Instinctively they looked around for his brass blunderbuss and saw it lying across the top of another barrel. Now, as he approached them, they could see he had two pistols tucked into the belt of his breeches, and they tried not to show their fear as he fixed them with his dark, hostile eyes, those same dark eyes that had put fear in their hearts the day he had accosted them on the way to Gracehill.

Expecting the worst, they stood before the outlaw and waited. Had he or one of his men seen them peeping around the corner of Mr Love's pighouse, they wondered? If so what would he do to them? Threaten them, shoot them, maybe even cut out their tongues to keep them from talking? Trembling, but trying not to show it, they kept their mouths shut as he walked over to them.

Thrusting out his broad chest in a manner which indicated that he may have been conscious of his lack of height, Archer regarded them. 'Haven't I seen you two somewhere before?' he asked.

This was it, they thought. Mr Love's farm, the murder. They were the only witnesses.

'Well, where was it?' he frowned. 'Ballymena maybe?'

Joshua and Sammy looked at one another. So he hadn't seen them at Mr Love's farm after all. A great feeling of relief surged through their bodies and they hoped it didn't show. At the same time, he knew he had seen them somewhere.

'That's right,' replied Sammy. 'It was in Ballymena – at the time of the rebellion.'

'We heard you making the speech at the Market House,' said Joshua, taking his cue.

'Aye, and a fine rousing speech it was,' added Sammy.

Joshua smiled and nodded vigorously to show that he agreed.

'And what were you doing at the Market House?' asked Archer.

'Looking for our fathers,' said Sammy.

'My father was wounded in the fighting,' said Joshua, giving the impression that he had been on the rebel side. 'but he's all right now.'

'And yours?'

'My father was arrested,' said Sammy.

'And where is he now?'

'I don't know,' replied Sammy truthfully, but giving the impression that perhaps he had been transported.

Just then, one of the men who had brought them to the cabin said, 'What about the cart, is it big enough?'

Archer nodded. 'Seems all right.'

'But that's our cart,' Joshua protested. 'What do you want it for?'

'We just want to borrow it for a while,' said Archer.

'And what do you want with us?' asked Sammy.

'Don't worry, no harm will come to you – provided you do what you're told.' Picking up his blunderbuss, he walked over to his horse, and pulled himself up into the saddle. As he swung around to go, he added, 'Consider yourselves the guests of the United Irishmen. Captain Nevin will look after you.'

Looking around, they saw the young freckle-faced sentry who had stopped them on the way to Gracehill, and then spoken up for them. He picked up his sword, which he had apparently left aside to do whatever work he had been doing with the barrel, and came over to them. He was smiling, and he asked them, 'Why did you not tell Tom where he had seen you?'

'Well, that day we met him, on the way to Gracehill,' said Sammy, 'he seemed to think we were spying on him, but we weren't. Really we weren't.'

'We were just on our way to the Moravian settlement,' added Joshua.

Captain Nevin nodded and assured them, 'All right. Don't worry about it.'

'What do you want with us,' asked Sammy. 'Why have you taken us prisoner?'

'You're not prisoners. As Tom said, you're our guests.'

'But what do you want us for?' asked Joshua.

The young rebel smiled and told them, 'You're going to help me to get to America.'

'How?' asked Sammy.

'In that barrel,' he replied.

'But you can't go to America in a barrel,' said Joshua. 'It's too far.'

Captain Nevin smiled again. 'No, but it'll take me part of the way – with your help.'

14

Dreams of an Exile

The men who were working at the barrel seemed to be measuring the inside of it, and strangely enough were doing so with the long pointed blade of a bayonet. Intrigued by this, Joshua and Sammy looked on. It was, they could see, a large oak barrel. It was bound with hoops of willow and had a circular wooden lid, like the ones that were delivered to the inn from the ale brewery.

'John,' said the man who was dipping the bayonet into the barrel, 'would you just sit in here again for a minute?'

Captain Nevin gave a good-natured sigh and smiled, 'Sure I'm only after getting out of it.'

'I know,' said the other man, 'but I want to be absolutely certain you'll be out of range if a militiaman pokes his bayonet into it.'

Gripping the rim of the barrel with both hands, Captain Nevin hopped up and disappeared down inside.

'Aye, that should do it,' said the other man. 'All right, out you get.'

'So that's it,' whispered Joshua. 'They're going to smuggle him out.'

'But they can't fill the top of it up with ale,' observed Sammy. 'The military would see what they were doing.'

Captain Nevin picked up his sword again and, almost as if he had heard them, said, 'We'll fill it up with corn. That way a bayonet won't go down too far, and they won't be able to see what we're up to?'

He draped his coat over his arm, put on his three-cornered hat and led them into the cabin. A small fire of peat glowed on the floor beneath the open chimney, and Joshua reckoned the rebels had lit it so that they could come in occasionally and warm themselves. No hens scurried from under their feet as they walked in and there was a dampness about the place which suggested it wasn't being lived in. Apart from a small table over at the back wall and several stools around the fire, it didn't have another piece of furniture. Nor was there any loft for sleeping in, but two heaps of straw had been spread out on the earthen floor and covered with rough blankets, indicating that some of the rebels may have spent a night there.

Captain Nevin put his coat down on one of the beds, and placed his sword on top of it. 'Get yourselves something to eat,' he said, motioning towards the table.

It was only then they realized that it was well into the afternoon. It was already beginning to get dark, and they were hungry. The food consisted of oaten bread and sweet milk, some of which they brought over to the fire where Captain Nevin was now sitting on a stool warming himself.

'Are they really going to smuggle you out in that barrel?' asked Sammy.

Captain Nevin smiled. 'Of course they are. There's a seat inside for me to sit on, and, once the false bottom is put in over my head, they'll fill the top up with corn. With a bit of luck the militia won't know the difference.'

'And where do we come into it?' asked Joshua.

'Well, we reckoned that if there was a young fellow sitting up at the front with the cart the militia would be less suspicious.'

'Which one?' asked Sammy, adding by way of explanation, 'Which one of us is going?'

Captain Nevin shrugged. 'It doesn't matter. We'll see when the time comes.'

'And what about the other one of us,' asked Joshua. 'I suppose you'll be holding him as hostage?'

Captain Nevin laughed. 'Not at all. Tom also has a journey to make, and he wants one of you to go with him.'

'You mean he's going to America too?' asked Sammy.

'Not at all. Tom says nobody will ever force him to leave his own country.'

Joshua was puzzled. 'Why are you going them?'

'Tom says I'm young enough to make a new start. He wants me to go.'

'And where exactly are you going in the barrel?' asked Joshua. 'You said it was taking you part of the way.'

Captain Nevin was leaning forward, with his arms on his knees, looking into the fire. 'It'll take me home first to see my family. I'm from the Ballymoney area, you know, just up the road. It'll probably be the last time I'll see them before I set sail.'

'And when will that be?' asked Sammy.

'Who knows? A month, maybe even a year. But whichever one of you goes with me, it'll only be part of the way. It'll have to be done in stages.'

'And when will we be allowed to go?' asked Joshua.

'You'll have to wait here for a couple of days until Tom gets word that I'm safely across the Bann. By that time I'll be in the mountains. The military will never find me there. Then it's just a matter of waiting.'

'Where's Mr Archer gone now?' asked Sammy.

'There's a young member of our group who's very ill. He's gone to see him.'

'But is that not dangerous?' asked Joshua.

Captain Nevin nodded. 'Of course it is. But he's very loyal to his men. He'd risk anything to see him.'

'Why did you do it anyway?' asked Joshua.

Captain Nevin looked at him. 'Why did I do what?'

'Why did you march on Ballymena? I mean, you and the other United Irishmen.'

Captain Nevin looked into the glowing fire again and sighed. 'I suppose you're too young to understand. But there were many reasons – many good reasons. You see, the whole system in this country is wrong. People are at odds with one another because of their religion. It was our hope in the Society of United Irishmen, that Catholic, Protestant and Dissenter could be united, leave all their differences behind, and be one people. Surely it can't be right that Presbyterians should have less rights than the Protestant Church, just because it's the official Church in this country, and that Catholics should have less rights than either of them.'

'I didn't know they had less rights,' said Sammy.

'Well they do,' Captain Nevin told him. 'Or at least they did. The Presbyterians aren't treated so badly now, but the Catholics still haven't got full emancipation.'

'That's something I never did understand,' said Joshua. 'Emancipation. What is it?'

'The right to vote,' Captain Nevin explained. 'Catholics got that six years ago, but they can only vote for somebody else. They're not allowed to stand for Parliament themselves, and yet they make up the majority of the population. Surely,' he added, 'we all should have the same rights.'

Both boys nodded. Even Joshua, who belonged to the official Church, couldn't argue with that.

'Then there's the discrimination that has left those poor wretches begging by the roadside,' Captain Nevin continued. 'They don't even have the right to eat.'

'And what religion are they?' asked Joshua.

'Religion?' said the captain. 'Who knows? They're just poor, the product of a rotten system.' He looked down between his knees at the earthen floor. 'The whole system's wrong. If a trading arrangement suits the interests of the British merchants, then the Parliament in London will support it. If it suits us, they won't do it, and all we get is hunger and poverty.' His face was getting flushed now from the fire, so he pushed back a bit. 'It was all of these things,' he explained by way of reply to Joshua's original question. 'All of these things, not just one of them, that led to the march on Ballymena, on Antrim, Down, Wicklow, Wexford and all the other places. We had the numbers but, unfortunately, not the training.'

There was silence and, to break the awkwardness of the moment, Sammy asked, 'How did you escape? I mean, after Colonel Clavering and his men arrived in the town?'

'Well, it's a funny thing,' said Captain Nevin. 'I don't know whether you believe in dreams or not, but if it hadn't been for a dream I had, I wouldn't be here today.'

'Why, what happened?' asked Sammy.

'When we were forced to abandon the town,' he recalled, 'myself and another United Irishman made our way back to the countryside and took refuge in the house of a friend. At least, we thought he was a friend. Whether it was tiredness or not, or maybe just the excitement, I don't know, but when I fell asleep I had this dream. I dreamt the yeomen had arrived at the house and were about to pounce on us and take us prisoner. I woke with a start and looked around, but there was nobody there. After a while I went back to sleep and would you believe it? I dreamt the very same thing. When I awoke again I was terrified. You know what it's like when you waken in the middle of the night like that.'

They nodded, thinking of the nights they had wakened after dreaming about the moiley cow, and he continued, 'I woke my friend and we decided to tell the owner of the house. I suppose we wanted to be reassured that we were worrying needlessly and that we were safe. You can imagine our reaction when his wife told us he wasn't at home. We knew that anyone who informed on us would receive a handsome reward, and we began to think that maybe our host wasn't the friend we thought he was. So we tried the door. It was securely fastened on the outside and we realized that he had locked us in while he had gone to fetch the military.'

'What did you do?' asked Joshua.

Captain Nevin smiled. 'What do you think? We grabbed our clothes and climbed out through the window as fast as we could. A short time later we heard the yeomen coming from the direction of Ballymena. We hid in a cornfield until the danger had passed, and then made good our escape. My friend also lives near Ballymoney, and soon afterwards the yeomen went to his father's house wanting

to know where his sons were. Another of his sons is a
United Irishman too, you see. Of course he couldn't tell
them, simply because he didn't know, so they burned his
house down.'

'Where's your friend now?' asked Joshua.

'He's going to America too. So's his brother.'

'And what happened the man you were staying with?'
asked Sammy.

'He got his reward all right, but not from the authorities. One night some of our friends took him from his bed
and gave him a good hazel-whipping, a lash for every mile
he rode to inform on us.'

Sammy and Joshua reckoned the young rebel captain
was being deliberately vague about some of the things he
was telling them. He had been careful not to name his
friend or say where he was now. Nor had he said who had
carried out the hazel-whipping on the informer, and they
wondered if perhaps Thomas Archer had had a hand in it.
But then, they thought, Archer would probably have shot
him.

'Is this your hide-out?' asked Sammy.

Captain Nevin shook his head. 'Tom would never bring
anyone to his hide-out. It would be more than his life was
worth. Even if he thinks someone knows where it is, he
gets very edgy.'

Joshua gave Sammy a knowing look. Was that why
Archer had threatened to shoot Mrs Dickey, he wondered?
And why he had shot Mr Love? Had they come to suspect
where he was hiding and threatened to tell?

'When are you going?' asked Joshua. 'I mean, in the
barrel?'

'Tomorrow, I hope.'

'Does that mean we have to stay here tonight?' asked
Sammy.

Captain Nevin nodded. 'I'm afraid so. But don't worry.
I'll see you come to no harm.'

'But why America?' asked Sammy.

'Why not?' The young rebel got up and, leaning on the half door with his arms, looked out into the gathering gloom. 'There's nothing here for me now, except perhaps the gallows. Even if they don't hang me, it's transportation. Somehow I don't fancy spending the rest of my life in Van Diemen's Land, or fighting for the King of Prussia against the army of France. Even worse, I might be sent overseas to serve in the British army. No, I'd rather take my chances in America.'

The other men had left at this stage, and, after looking around outside to check for any danger, Captain Nevin bolted the door and built up a good fire to keep them warm. Fortunately, their bed was a little bit away from his and later, when he had fallen asleep, they were able to talk to each other, albeit in whispers.

'Why were you afraid to tell Archer that we met him on the way to Gracehill?' asked Joshua.

'Because then he might remember forcing my father to join the rebels.'

'So?'

'Well, if he found out he was arrested and released, he might think he was an informer.'

Joshua didn't quite follow his friend's thinking, so he just whispered, 'I'm not surprised he didn't recognize us. I'm filthy from working around the farm. So are my clothes.' He pulled his coat up around his neck to keep himself warm, then reached down and felt the hem to make sure the button of the Dunseverick Cavalry was still tucked safely inside. 'Do you think the military will be out looking for us?'

'How could they?' asked Sammy. 'Your uncle won't know we haven't arrived home, and our folks won't know we've left.'

'You're right,' said Joshua. 'We're not due home for another week. Do you think maybe we should try and escape?'

'Sure, where would we go? We don't know where we are.'

'That's true,' said Joshua. 'And even if we did make it back into town, they might think we were going to fetch the military. And you know what they'd do to us then.'

Sammy agreed. 'Aye, we'd be lucky to get away with a hazel-whipping.'

'They'd probably cut our tongues out,' said Joshua. 'Maybe even kill us, the way they killed Mr Love.'

'Shush ...' whispered Sammy. 'If they find out we saw that we're really done for.'

Gradually they drifted off into an uneasy sleep, but unlike the dreams Captain Nevin had had, there was nothing in theirs to suggest that the military might be coming to get them, and when at long last morning came they knew there was no possibility that they would be coming.

Even though they were now in the second week of December, it was a mild morning. A wintry sun was coming out from behind the clouds and the plaintive call of a peewit floated across the landscape from a distance that seemed to underline their isolation.

'Well, John,' said Archer to Captain Nevin, 'It won't be long now.'

The other rebels had returned and were working at the barrel again. Joshua and Sammy watched for a while, then asked if they could tend to Matthew's horse.

'The horse is fine,' Captain Nevin assured them. 'I fed it myself last night, and again this morning.' He smiled. 'If my life's going to depend on it, the least I can do is make sure it's fed and watered.'

They leaned back against a large stone to catch what little warmth there was in the sun, and, as Captain Nevin lifted his sword so that he wouldn't be sitting on it, Joshua asked him, 'Can I see it?'

'Of course you can,' he replied, and drawing it from the scabbard, sliced the air to show how effective it could be. 'It's really a sabre,' he explained. 'That's why it's curved.'

'What's the difference?' asked Sammy.

'A straight one is for sword-fighting. This is for slashing at your enemy when you're on horseback.' He sliced the air with it again to demonstrate, and added, 'But you could use it for sword-fighting too, if you wanted. Come on, I'll show you.'

They followed him around to the front of the cabin, and over to a clump of sally bushes.

'Did you ever use it? I mean for sword-fighting?' asked Joshua.

'Not really. It's more for show than anything else.' He cut off a couple of fairly straight branches. 'And it's good for chopping things too!'

'Now,' he said, handing one of the sticks to Sammy, 'Defend yourself.'

Pretending that he was wielding a sword, Sammy thrust at one side of the sabre, then the other.

With a broad smile on his face, Captain Nevin parried each thrust, taking care to hold the sabre upright in a way that posed no danger to his young opponent.

'Let me try,' said Joshua, seeing that it could be great fun.

Joshua now thrust his stick at the upright sabre, Sammy joined in and in a few moments Captain Nevin had backed himself up against the cabin wall. 'All right, all right,' he cried in mock surrender. 'I give in.'

'Now,' he said, sliding the sabre back down into its scabbard, 'you can say you've crossed swords with a United Irishman.'

'No we won't,' Joshua assured him. 'We won't tell anybody. Honest we won't.'

Captain Nevin nodded. 'Good.'

When they followed him back around to the yard, they found that the men had yoked the horse to the cart, and were in the process of hoisting the barrel into the back.'

'Time to go,' Archer told him. 'And don't forget – say hello to the land of liberty for me.'

Captain Nevin smiled and nodded, saying, 'I will. I'll say it for all of you.'

For a moment the two embraced, then the younger man pulled himself up into the cart and climbed into the barrel. The false bottom was fitted above his head and the remaining space filled with corn.

As the lid was fitted into place, Archer turned to Sammy and said, 'All right, up you go. And if the military stop you, let our man do the talking.'

The driver gave a flick of the reins and, to the waves and best wishes of the others, the young rebel captain set off on the bumpy road to Ballymoney and America.

For his part, Sammy didn't know where the first stage of the journey would take them and he knew there was no point in asking. He was also wondering how he was going to get back to the cabin when the driver told him, 'Any sign of the redcoats, knock three times on the barrel to alert Captain Nevin. Otherwise, leave things to me. I'll do the talking.'

Sammy nodded. Guests of the outlaws they might be, but he knew that as long as Joshua was being held at the cabin he had no option but to keep his mouth shut and do as he was told.

As they made their way along one track, then another, Sammy wondered if they would rejoin the main road at the same place, and what would happen if Matthew spotted them going past.

Matthew might not recognise him, seeing that he was with an adult, but he would certainly recognise the horse and cart. If he did, he would know immediately that something was wrong and draw his pistol. If that happened, the United Irishman would draw his too, and one of them was bound to be killed.

These worries were going through Sammy's head when they emerged on to the main road, and it was with a great sense of relief that he realized they had come out well north of Matthew's farm. Now all he had to worry about

A challenge from the militia

was the military. A meeting with them could mean a
shoot-out too, and he himself would be a target.

Now and then Captain Nevin's muffled voice could be
heard coming from the barrel, telling the driver to take it
easy whenever they hit a rut in the road, or inquiring
about their progress.

One particularly bad patch of road brought a yelp of
pain from inside the barrel and Sammy was about to ask
Captain Nevin if he was all right when the driver
muttered, 'Redcoats!'

Looking up, Sammy saw that two militiamen had
stepped out on to the road, as they rounded a bend. Their
long muskets were at the ready, their bayonets fixed to the
end of them.

Fearing that the militiamen might have heard the howl
of pain from the barrel, Sammy held on to his hat and
shouted, 'Take it easy.' At the same time he knocked on
the barrel three times and hoped Captain Nevin would get
the message.

As the cart came to a standstill, one of the soldiers
approached and asked, 'Who are you and what's your
business?'

'I'm a farmer,' the driver replied. 'I'm making a delivery
to the military in Ballymoney.'

'A delivery of what?' asked the soldier, climbing up on
to the cart.

'Corn,' said the driver. 'It's for their horses.'

The soldier prized off the lid of the barrel, and taking up
a handful of grain let it run through his fingers.

'It was a bad harvest,' said the driver, 'but I was lucky.
It's in short supply, even for the army.'

'Who ordered it?' asked the soldier.

'I can't remember his name,' said the driver. 'But he said
they'd meet us half way. You're not them by any chance?'

The soldier shook his head and dug his hand deeper
into the barrel.

'Well, would you take it and give it to them when you

see them?'

The soldier promptly replaced the lid on the barrel, saying, 'It's nothing to do with us.' He hopped back out on to the road, and added, 'We're foot soldiers. If they said they'd meet you, they'll have a cart.'

Sammy smiled. He could see that the driver's ploy had worked. The soldiers weren't prepared to hang around, possibly for hours, just to facilitate the cavalry. From remarks he had overheard in the town, he knew the foot soldiers disliked the cavalry, apparently because they thought anyone on horseback had a much easier life than anyone who had to walk.

Waved on by the unsuspecting soldiers, they continued their journey. Several miles further on, they turned right off the main road and didn't stop until they arrived at a small stone cabin overlooking a lake. There several men were waiting with another cart and a fresh horse.

Jumping down, Sammy watched as the men scooped out the corn and extracted Captain Nevin from the barrel. He was obviously very cramped, but, after walking around for a few minutes and stretching his legs, he announced that he was fine.

The cabin was a very primitive structure, with sods on the roof and no chimney for a fire. However, the men had laid in food for their visitors, and after they had eaten Captain Nevin announced that he was ready for the next leg of his journey. By this time his helpers had transferred the barrel to the other cart, and, having shaken hands with all of them, he shook hands with Sammy. 'Give my regards to the brethren in God's acre,' he whispered, with a knowing wink.

Sammy smiled and promised he would. Minutes later he was sitting in the back of their own cart, and as they drew away from the cabin he could see Captain Nevin climbing back into the barrel. He smiled again and whispered to himself, 'Give my regards to America.'

15

Running the Gauntlet

It was early morning, and a cold blast of air came in through the door when Thomas Archer arrived at the cabin. Leaving his brass blunderbuss on the table, he walked over to the fire where he sat down on one of the stools to warm himself. During the night the temperature had dropped, and Joshua and Sammy had heard one of the men who had been left to guard them getting up and putting sods of peat on the fire to give them more heat. Had it not been for that, they reckoned they would have frozen to death, for dawn revealed that a hard frost had set in, freezing the puddles and turning the willows a Christmassy white.

Joshua went to the table and ran his fingers over the wooden butt of the blunderbuss, then the brass barrel. The wood was polished from continuous handling, the brass not as cold as he expected metal to be. 'Is it all right if I lift it?' he asked without turning around.

'Go ahead,' said Archer. 'It's not loaded.'

Taking up the gun, Joshua found to his surprise that it was very well balanced, the wooden butt being about the same length as the barrel. Overall, he could see, it was much longer than a pistol, yet much shorter than a musket. Sturdy, powerful, yet almost comfortable to handle, he could understand why an outlaw like Archer might become very attached to it.

'I see it says it was made in Dublin.'

'That's right,' said Archer. '1760.'

Joshua handed the gun to Sammy who looked at the flintlock mechanism above the trigger and asked, 'How does it work?'

Archer came over to them and, taking the gun, explained, 'This catch holds the bayonet.' He curled his forefinger around it and when he pulled it back the long sharp dagger-like blade that was folded along the top of the barrel flicked forward.

Sammy and Joshua exchanged glances and thought of the day the outlaw had flicked it into their faces on the way to Gracehill.

Archer folded the bayonet back, secured it again with the catch, and laid the gun down on the table. 'This is the ammunition,' he told them, and taking five lead balls from his coat pocket, wrapped them in a piece of old linen.

'Why are you putting them in that?' asked Joshua.

Standing the gun upright on the table, Archer proceeded to pour the contents of a powder flask into the barrel. 'First the gunpowder,' he said, 'then the shot.' He dropped the lethal packet of lead balls into the barrel, and explained, 'The linen's to keep them from falling back out again.' He extracted a short rod which, they could see, was fitted to the underside of the barrel and used it to ram the lead balls home. Then he picked up a piece of old newspaper from the table and rammed that down the barrel too. 'Now you see,' he said, pointing the barrel at the floor, 'the shot doesn't fall out.'

'And how does it work?' asked Sammy. 'I mean, what makes it fire?'

'See this small hole in the side of the barrel?' Archer, pointed to the end nearest the trigger. 'That's the touch-hole. I pour some powder into the small pan beside it and when I pull the trigger, the flint flies forward, sending sparks into the powder. The flame goes through the hole, the powder inside the barrel ignites, and BANG.'

Startled, they both stepped back and, for the first time, saw a smile flicker across the dark face of the outlaw. 'Now,' he told Joshua, and the smile was gone. 'It's time we were on our way.'

'When will you be back?' asked Sammy.

Archer was already on his way out. 'Not before night-fall,' he replied. One of his men was waiting outside with his horse, and without another word he pulled himself into the saddle, helped Joshua up behind him, and galloped off.

Weak through the wintry sun was, it was now beginning to release the countryside from its icy grip. Holding his blunderbuss across his lap with one hand, Archer guided his horse with the other, taking them through a maze of country lanes, across fields, around swamps, over bogs and into woods, in a path that he had obviously used before but which only he himself knew. Not once did they see the red coat of a militiaman or the curious eye of a peasant peeping over a half door. The only creature to witness their passing was an occasional snipe, which rose with a shriek and spiralled into the cold blue sky.

As they jogged along, Archer didn't speak, and Joshua was left to his own thoughts. He wondered where they were going, what they were going to do when they got there, and what his part in it was going to be. But, above all, he kept wondering what his mother and father would say if they could see him now, riding across the countryside behind the infamous outlaw, Thomas Archer. The same outlaw who featured on posters all over the town, the most wanted man in the north, perhaps in all of Ireland, the man every soldier in the county was looking for.

They had been riding for about two hours, when Archer asked him if he was hungry and, without waiting for a reply, reached him a piece of bread. He was hungry all right, and cramped and sore, but he didn't complain. He didn't dare.

Eventually they came to another bog, and for the first time, Joshua thought it looked familiar. He was trying to figure out where they were when Archer nudged the horse into a sprawling patch of sallies and told him to dismount.

Having tied the reins to a sally branch, the outlaw growled, 'Wait here.' Then, bending down, he disappeared into the tangle of scrub.

A dangerous journey

Joshua watched and waited. He still hadn't figured out where they were and, when Archer didn't return, he decided to follow him. The undergrowth was thick and long arching briars tore at his coat but he persevered. A few minutes later he found himself looking out at a small thatched cottage in the middle of a clearing. A man was gathering up an armful of firewood at the gable end, and when he looked around Joshua knew immediately who he was. It was Jemmy O'Brien, the chandler. Now he realized why the bog had looked familiar. It was the Star Bog at Galgorm Parks, not far from Gracehill.

For a moment Joshua thought of calling out to Mr O'Brien for help, but changed his mind. It occurred to him, just as it had on the day Sammy had called at the cottage for rope, that Mr O'Brien wouldn't take too kindly to him on account of the fact that he was barred from the inn. More important, the outlaws were still holding Sammy back at the cabin and he couldn't do anything that would put his friend's life in danger.

Quickly retracing his steps, he emerged from the bushes only to find that Archer had got there before him.

'I thought I told you to stay here?' said the outlaw.

'I, ah …' Joshua mumbled, indicating that he had just answered a call of nature.

'All right. But next time I tell you to do something, do it.'

Joshua could see that Archer had gone into the bushes to get a bundle of clothes, and when they had mounted up again he held these in his lap, with the blunderbuss resting across them, ready as always for any emergency.

Now Joshua knew where they were going. They were heading for Ballymena. But why? Why should Archer risk such a visit? The town was full of soldiers, and if he was caught it would mean certain death.

In the woods at the edge of the town, Archer stopped again, took off his swallow-tailed coat and hid it in the undergrowth. Then he opened the bundle and started putting on the other clothes. To his amazement, Joshua saw that they were women's clothes. Furthermore, the outlaw was putting them on over his shirt and breeches so that he looked like a short, fat woman.

'Now,' he said, tying the strings of a bonnet under his stubbly chin. 'Who would ever think that I was Archer the outlaw?' He pulled a cloak around his shoulders and picking up his blunderbuss, tucked it underneath.

Joshua was speechless. The light was beginning to fade, and there was no doubt about it; no one would ever suspect that this little woman was the outlaw who had been terrifying the countryside for the past two years. Especially since she was accompanied by her rather ragged and dirty son! Now Joshua knew why he had been brought along. But what was the purpose of their visit?

He was on the point of asking, when Archer said, 'I'm going up to Castle Street to see my parents. If any of the soldiers stop us, you do the talking. Tell them your mother has lost her voice and that we're searching the inns for your father. Say he's a terrible man for the drink. They'll accept that.'

Joshua nodded and off they went. He wondered what he would do if they went up by Mill Street and passed his father's inn. What if his father recognized him? Or Moses? Or Naomi? That might alert the soldiers, and if Archer produced his blunderbuss somebody was bound to get hurt. Then Sammy would be in trouble, when the other outlaws heard what had happened.

Fortunately, Archer decided to avoid the centre of the town. Instead, he cut through the Shambles, hurried across Bridge Street and made his way along a narrow, twisting alley, which Joshua knew would bring them up on to Castle Street. It was obvious that the outlaw knew every inch of the town, but then, thought Joshua, that was hardly surprising. As a boy, he would have explored every nook and cranny.

It was almost dark now and candles were burning in the

windows when they looked out into Castle Street, which ran from the Market House up to the gates of the Adair Demesne. It was from the stately home of the Adairs that the street had got its name, and its proximity to the seat of power in the area had also made it an appropriate place for the military to establish their headquarters. Because of this, soldiers were always coming and going, thus making the outlaw's visit even more dangerous, but now that the curfew had been lifted none of them took the slightest notice of the woman and boy who hurried past.

Further up the street, opposite the military headquarters, two soldiers chatted to several young women of the town. It was their job to take a note of anyone of interest who went near the Archer home. For the moment, however, the young women were of more interest to them than the women and boy who now approached the cottage. As a result, they barely looked around when the woman knocked at the door and hurried inside. Nor did they pay any attention to the boy or wonder why he lounged around outside.

Sliding to the ground, Joshua huddled up against the white-washed wall and put his arms around his legs for warmth. He could hear the soldiers joking and talking, while the girls giggled as they vied with each other for the young men's attention. It was dark, and he could barely make them out in the light of a nearby window, but he could tell by the way they were talking that the soldiers weren't even looking in his direction. Gradually he relaxed, and thought of his own home down beyond the Market House. How strange, he thought, that he should be sitting on the side of the cold street, acting as look-out for an outlaw, while less than a hundred yards away his family were probably enjoying a nice warm fire.

He was deep in his thoughts when someone kicked him and demanded, 'What are you doing here?'

Startled, he looked up to see a militiaman pointing a musket at him.

'Ah, it's my father,' he said, thinking desperately for an excuse. 'He's a terrible man for the drink. My mother sent me to fetch him home.'

'All right,' said the militiaman, 'but you'll have to move on.' He nudged him with the muzzle of the gun. 'We don't like people hanging around here.'

'Right,' said Joshua, getting to his feet. 'I'll wait for him down the street.'

The soldier turned and disappeared into the darkness. From the laughs and giggles that were coming from the opposite side of the street, Joshua could tell that the other two soldiers were still too busy to notice him. Sidling up to the window of the cottage, he tapped gently but urgently on the window. A few minutes later Archer was beside him, his visit over, and together they hurried away into the night.

It had occurred to Joshua that no matter how well Archer knew the countryside he wouldn't be able to find his way back to the cabin in darkness, at least not by the same route. And he would hardly chance going back by road as there was no telling when he would run into soldiers. Archer himself didn't discuss the matter with him. Indeed, he said very little, but when they had made their way to a point about three miles from the town, they stopped at another cabin. It wasn't Jemmy O'Brien's, nor was it one Joshua could identify. Dismounting, Archer knocked on the door with his knuckle, a coded knock, it seemed to Joshua. A password was whispered back and forth, and a few minutes later a man ushered them inside.

No candle had been lit and after a few whispered words the man retreated into the darkness. Joshua got the impression that the members of his family were asleep in the corner, perhaps even sitting up on a bed of straw, wondering what was going on. If they were there they didn't say anything. Archer sat down with his back against the wall on one side of the fireplace and, leaving his blunderbuss on the hearth beside him, indicated to Joshua that he should rest on the other side. The fire was almost dead and Joshua was grateful for the little heat that remained in the wall behind him. Wrapping himself up in his coat, he closed his eyes, knowing that the tiredness of the day would eventually overcome the discomfort of the night.

Dawn hadn't yet arrived when Archer shook Joshua and told him they must be on their way. He was stiff and sore from sleeping on the earthen floor. He was also hungry, but somehow he knew that when daylight came there would be other, younger, mouths in the cabin in greater need of food than he was, and he just hoped they would get it.

A few hours later, Archer and Joshua arrived back at the thatched cabin. Some of the men had boiled a pot of potatoes and never did Joshua find the heat of the fire more welcome or the smell of potatoes more appetising.

'Where were you?' whispered Sammy when his friend walked in.

'I'll tell you later,' said Joshua out of the corner of his mouth.

Having warmed himself briefly at the fire, Archer joined his men at the table. As well as the potatoes, they had got more milk from somewhere, and a pat of butter. Everyone got a share, not least Joshua and Sammy who were sitting at the fire, and for a while it seemed the need to satisfy their hunger was more important than talking.

'That was great,' whispered Joshua at last. 'I wonder where they got the potatoes?'

'Where do you think?' Sammy whispered back. 'From our cart. Where else?'

'Well, I don't care,' said Joshua. 'I was famished.'

Archer got up and went out and his men followed.

'Where were you?' Sammy asked again.

Joshua scooped up the scattered remains of the potatoes from the bottom of the pot and ate them out of his hand. 'Castle Street. We were up at Castle Street. He went to see his parents.'

'You mean you were in the town? And what about the military? How come they didn't spot him?'

Joshua rested his elbows on his knees and held his hands up to the fire. Sammy's usually pale face, he could see, was red from the heat. 'You won't believe it,' he said and went on to tell Sammy everything that had happened.

'It was very daring, wasn't it?' said Sammy when Joshua had finished. 'I mean, dressing up as a woman and walking right up to his own house.'

Joshua nodded. 'He took an awful chance.'

'Captain Nevin said he was very loyal all right,' said Sammy, adding in case Joshua might interpret the remark in the wrong way. 'I mean, to his family and friends.'

Joshua agreed. 'Aye, he's loyal all right, as long as you're loyal to him. But I wouldn't like to cross him.'

Just then Archer came back in. 'I'm going now,' he told them gruffly.

'When are you going to let us go?' asked Sammy.

'As soon as I get word that Captain Nevin is safely across the Bann.'

'How will you know?' asked Joshua.

'I'll know.'

'And how will we know?' asked Sammy.

'You'll know,' was all the outlaw would tell them, and without another word he turned and left.

It remained cold all day, and they didn't stray far from the cabin. By nightfall it became apparent that only two of Archer's men remained to keep guard on them, and when they awoke next morning they discovered that they were alone in the cabin.

Scrambling to his feet, Joshua threw open the half door. 'The horse and cart,' he cried. 'They're outside.'

Sammy was beside him in an instant, and together they walked around to the back yard. It was deserted.

'They've gone,' said Joshua. 'They must have got word.'

Sammy was looking into the back of the cart. 'The

potatoes,' he said. 'And the vegetables. They've put them back.'

Joshua nodded, wondering at the strange logic of it all, but only for a moment. 'Come on,' he said. 'Let's go while the going's good.'

Sammy needed no second bidding. Together they climbed up on to the cart, and, whether it was the urgent flick of the reins or the even more urgent click of their tongues that spurred the horse into a gallop, it wasn't long before they had left the cabin far behind. Nor did they know if they followed the same route back to the road, or indeed how they found it, but find it they did and it was with a great sense of relief that they resumed their journey home.

'One thing for sure,' said Sammy when they had composed themselves. 'I'm never going to breathe a word about this to living soul.'

'Me neither,' said Joshua. 'I don't want to end up like Mr Love.'

'Or the man from Clough,' Sammy reminded him. 'Imagine! Cutting off his tongue to keep him from talking.'

'For a while there, I didn't think they were going to let us go,' said Joshua.

'And why did they, do you think?'

Joshua shrugged. 'Why not? We don't know where their real hide-out is. And who knows where Captain Nevin is now?'

Sammy agreed. 'Or what ship he'll get to America, if he ever gets one.'

'I hope he makes it,' said Joshua. 'You know, I liked him.'

Sammy looked over at his friend and smiled. 'So did I.'

16

A Piece of Silver

The black coach had drawn up beside Dickey's mansion and behind the closed door of the captain's study the secret world of military intelligence was once again being discussed at Hillhead.

'Christmas has come and gone,' complained Captain Dickey. He was standing with his back to the fire, his hands clasped behind his back, a posture that was meant to convey his impatience as clearly as anything he might say.

As always, the visitor sat in the shadows and the light from the fire that occasionally flickered across his face did little to tell Captain Dickey what his thoughts might be.

'We're now in the year 1800,' he went on, 'and we're still no nearer to apprehending them.'

'I wouldn't quite say that,' replied his visitor. 'As a matter of fact, my men have made significant progress.'

'Progress? What progress?'

'Within a very short time, I hope to have our esteemed Dr Linn in our grasp.' Captain Dickey was about to say something, but was silenced by a gesture of his visitor's hand. 'And that's not all. Our young friend Roddy Mc-Corley should be joining us soon too.'

'You mean you actually expect to arrest them?' asked Captain Dickey.

His visitor nodded. 'And with a little luck, one or two others.'

'But this is great news,' beamed the captain. Lifting a bottle of brandy from the table, he poured a glass for his visitor, then one for himself, and relaxing into an armchair said, 'I'll drink to that.'

They touched glasses and savoured the brandy as it trickled warmly down their gullets.

'But what about Archer?' continued Captain Dickey. 'When are we going to get him?'

'All in good time,' replied his visitor. 'All in good time.'

'But when?' repeated Captain Dickey. 'So long as he's at large, the liberty tree will never be completely rooted out.'

His visitor learned forward and, for the first time, Captain Dickey saw a smile flicker across his face.

'Information has come my way,' he confided, 'that Archer has been known to call at a cabin on the edge of the Star Bog in the townland of Galgorm. . . '

'I know where it is,' said Captain Dickey. 'Go on.'

'That cabin is occupied by a man called Jemmy O'Brien.'

'O'Brien, the chandler?' interrupted the captain again. 'Why, the good-for-nothing. . . '

'Anyway,' his visitor continued, 'I've made what you might call a little arrangement.'

'You mean, with O'Brien? It's a rope that blackguard should be getting, not a reward.'

His visitor sat back again, as if retreating into the shadows. 'I didn't say my informant was Jemmy O'Brien. But even if it was, the reward and the person who receives it are of little consequence compared with the prize that is to be won.'

Captain Dickey nodded. 'Quite so. Quite so.'

'As a matter of fact,' his visitor went on, 'the arrangement I have made involves a woman.'

'A woman?' Captain Dickey seemed surprised.

'Yes, a woman. And a shopkeeper.'

Captain Dickey filled up the glasses and leaned forward to hear more.

'The arrangement I have made is this.' The visitor crossed his legs and sipped his brandy again. 'When the woman presents a certain coin to the shopkeeper here in town – the coin has an identifying mark upon it, you understand – it will be the signal that Archer is at

O'Brien's cabin. I will be informed immediately and then it is up to you and your men to do the rest.'

'And so we shall,' declared Captain Dickey. He got to his feet as if to illustrate that he was ready for action and, raising his glass, repeated, 'So we shall.'

His visitor got up to go. 'I'll give you more precise details later. In the meantime say nothing of this to anyone. For if Archer forms the slightest suspicion that we are setting a trap for him, someone will surely die.'

It was Jimmy the Post who made the historic announcement. February had come and people were still getting used to the New Year, when Jimmy, in a rare display of energy, waved Mr Watson's paper in the air, and proclaimed that the Parliament in Dublin had voted in favour of the Union.

'What does he mean, the union?' asked Naomi who had come out with her mother from the back of the inn.

'The union of Ireland and Britain,' said Mrs Watson.

The word spread quickly and people crowded into the inn to hear more.

Mr Watson opened the paper and cast his eye over the dispatches from Dublin. 'It's true,' he told them. 'Both Houses of Parliament there received the king's recommendation for a legislative union from the lord lieutenant. The message from the king said union unquestionably was the common interest of both his kingdoms.'

'What does it mean, both houses of Parliament?' asked one man.

'The House of Commons and the House of Lords,' another, more informed man, told him.

'And have they voted for it?' inquired yet another.

'They have,' said Mr Watson. 'Both Houses have agreed to it.'

'Does that mean the union has taken place?' asked Naomi.

Mr Watson shook his head. 'No. They've just agreed to
the king's message. I suppose they'll have to pass it as a
Bill at some stage, making it official.'

After a while, the crowd went their various ways, knots
of people talking among themselves as they tried to
understand the implications of it all. Mr and Mrs Watson
also discussed it at length, but it wasn't until Joshua came
home from school that he heard the news.

'Will it be a good thing, this union?' he asked, lifting his
head from his homework.

Mrs Watson, who was sitting in her favourite chair beside the fire, hesitated, 'Some say it will,' she told him.
'Some say it won't. I don't know.'

Joshua thought this was odd, coming from a person who
was so devoted to the Crown, but then he had seen enough
during the rebellion to know that when it came to Irish
politics nothing seemed to be simple or straightforward.

'But why?' asked Joshua. 'I mean, why now?'

'It's because of the rebellion, stupid,' said Naomi, who
had listened to everything her parents had said.

'What do you know about it?' retorted Joshua. 'Anyway,
you're supposed to have a cold. But you'll be well able for
school tomorrow.'

Mrs Watson intervened to calm things down and Joshua
resumed his homework. Or at least, he tried to resume it.
He was still trying to work out what union would mean. It
probably *was* because of the rebellion, he thought, but he
wouldn't please Naomi to say so. Maybe his teacher
would tell them more about it. Somehow, with the arrival
of the new teacher and the resumption of school, the
rebellion seemed to have been forgotten. However, this
move towards a union of the two countries showed clearly
that it had not been forgotten. Nor, he was soon to learn,
had the leaders who were still at large.

Timmy Corr and Matty Meek were sitting on the
parapet of the hump-backed bridge across the River Braid
at the lower end of the town, when they saw the scarlet

tunics of soldiers coming from the direction of Randalstown and Toome. On the look-out, as ever, for something
foolish to do, and unaware that they were watching an
event that some would sing about for centuries to come,
they hopped down off the parapet and hurried forward to
join the procession.

The soldiers, they found, were escorting a prisoner into
town. He was young, hatless and fair-haired. His hands
were bound behind his back, and he was being led by a
rope that was tied in a noose around his neck.

Greeting the soldiers, as he greeted everyone, with a call
of 'Hi, Jackie,' Timmy waited until the procession had
passed, then fell in behind. His head thrown back, he
marched beside his small friend all the way up to the
military headquarters in Castle Street. Both were
beaming, blissfully unaware that the soldiers had captured
one of the leaders of the battle of Antrim.

Soon everyone in town was talking about the prisoner,
and as Joshua made his way from school, he heard people
discussing who it might be. They had various descriptions
and as many theories, but one remark in particular stuck
in his mind. 'All I know,' he heard one old woman saying,
'is that he was a young fella. And he had fair hair.' He
immediately thought of Captain Nevin, and wondered if,
perhaps, he hadn't succeeded in getting aboard a sailing
ship after all.

'Is it true?' he asked his father breathlessly.

His father was busy in the inn as usual. 'Is what true?'

'That they've got one of the United leaders?'

'It is,' said his father, and continued to do what he was
doing.

'Who is he?' asked Joshua, hardly wanting to hear the
answer.

'Young McCorley from Toome. Why?'

Relieved to hear it wasn't Captain Nevin, Joshua lowered his voice. 'He's one of the men we met that day on the
way to Gracehill. The one Archer called Roddy.'

'*A most awful procession*'

His father nodded. 'That's him all right and, mark my words, the others won't be long after him.'

Mr Watson was right. Word now reached them that the military had arrested several more, including the rebel known as Dr Linn.

'It's only a matter of time, all right,' grunted Moses, 'before they have them all.' He was rubbing down one of the cart horses and Joshua and Sammy had come in to give him a hand.

'What do you think they'll do with them?' asked Sammy.

'Do with them?' The old man looked at him in a way that suggested it was a silly question.

'Well, what I mean is,' said Sammy, 'do you think maybe they'll transport them?'

Moses shook his head. 'Not these ones.'

'You think then, they'll hang them?' asked Joshua.

'I don't think it,' said Moses, giving the horse a final rub along the back. 'I know it.'

Because Joshua had to go to school, and Sammy had to work, they didn't see the procession that took Roddy McCorley out of the town to his place of execution. Their elders were also reluctant to discuss it, so it wasn't until they got hold of the *News-Letter* the following Tuesday that they learned more about it.

Joshua spread the paper out on the floor of the loft above the stables and Sammy listened intently as he read it out.

'It says: "Extract of a letter from Ballymena, Sunday, 2nd March. Upon Friday last, a most awful procession took place here, namely the escorting of Roger McCorley, who was lately convicted at a court martial, to the place of execution, Toome Bridge, the unfortunate man having been bred in that neighbourhood..." '

'Go on,' urged Sammy. 'What else does it say?'

'It says his body was given up to dissection, and after-wards buried under the gallows.'

'What does that mean?' asked Sammy.

'I don't know. I suppose they must have cut him up. Anyway ... listen to this.' Joshua shifted to make himself more comfortable. ' "Tomorrow Caskey" – he's one of the others – "will be executed at Ahoghill, and upon Tuesday, the celebrated Dr Linn at Randalstown. Thus, of late, we have got rid of six of those nefarious wretches, who have kept this neighbourhood in the greatest misery for some time past." '

'Does it say anything about Archer?' asked Sammy.

'No. But wait ... down here. Listen: "In consequence of some information given by those unhappy men, there is reason to believe the noted Archer will soon be in our guard-room ... " '

'Did you tell anybody about meeting Archer and his men out at Kildowney,' whispered Sammy.

Joshua shook his head. 'Nobody. Not even my parents.'

'Me neither,' said Sammy. He picked up the paper. 'It's funny isn't it? The paper says Dr Linn will be executed on Tuesday, and by the time we get it, it's already happened. What time do you think they did it at?'

'Probably this morning.'

'Then the military should be coming back from Randalstown soon,' said Sammy. 'Why don't we go down as far as the bridge and wait for them?'

'Right, but first I'd better leave the paper back, or my father will kill me.'

When they reached the bridge, they learned from others who had gathered there that the soldiers had already returned from their grim task. They had nothing else to do, so they stayed and, a short time later, they saw a contingent of yeomen under the command of Captain Dickey marching out towards Gracehill. The yeomen were accompanied by a party of regular troops, and there was an urgency in their step that made some onlookers wonder where they were going. The older people waited until the scarlet tunics had disappeared up the winding road, then headed home for their tea. Had they known the purpose of Captain Dickey's march, they would have stayed.

'I don't know about you,' said Sammy, 'but if I go back in now I'm going to get a job to do.'

Joshua nodded. 'Me too.'

For a while they messed around at the river, building small mud harbours and floating pieces of wood which they pretended were ships. Taking one of them in his hand, Sammy sent it sailing out into the river, where it was caught by the current and quickly swept out of sight. 'Guess where that one's going?' he said.

Joshua smiled. 'America.'

After a time they tired of the game and climbed back up to the road. They were dusting themselves down when a man galloped in from the direction of Gracehill on a cart-horse. He was riding bareback, and was breathless with the news he was bringing to the town.

'They're searching the Star Bog,' he announced.

'What for?' asked Sammy.

'I don't know.' He spurred his horse forward and galloped on up towards the Market House, calling back over his shoulder, 'Probably one of the outlaws.'

Joshua and Sammy looked at one another, each wondering the same thing. 'Come on,' said Joshua, and without another word they set out at a fast trot on the road to Gracehill.

The month of March had brought a good stretch in the evenings and it was still bright when they came across a group of soldiers on the road.

The soldiers had their muskets at the ready and refused to let them pass.

'But why not?' asked Joshua. 'We're not doing any harm.'

'The whole area's surrounded,' one of the soldiers informed them. 'Nobody's allowed in – or out.'

'But why?' asked Sammy.

'Archer the outlaw,' said the soldier. 'We've got him

surrounded in the Star Bog.'

Casually, Joshua and Sammy turned and went back the way they had come, but as soon as they were around a corner and out of sight they left the road and hurried through the woods in the direction of the Star Bog.

It wasn't until they approached Jemmy O'Brien's cabin that they came across more troops. Soldiers on horseback, they could see, had surrounded the bog and were waiting with sabres at the ready, while foot soldiers fanned out across it and, with bayonets fixed to their muskets, were prodding every mound of heather and tussock of grass.

Captain Dickey was in the thick of it, his water-spaniel running around sniffing the scents, and every now and then raising its dark brown head to see where it was going. One or two other people who lived in cabins on the edge of the bog also watched, but, like Joshua and Sammy, were ever aware of the horses beside them, and the gleaming silver sabres held upright in the gloved hands of the horsemen.

After a while the scarlet tunics faded into the distance, then slowly came back into focus as the soldiers searched the bog again on the way back. The onlookers moved their feet to prevent the water creeping up around them, while the horses, which were positioned on firmer ground, lowered their heads and snorted with impatience.

It was getting cold now. The foot soldier's were wet and tired and one of the first to return told the cavalrymen, 'No sign of him.' The cavalrymen pulled their horses around, and were about to leave when someone shouted, 'Here he is! Over here!' The other soldiers immediately turned, and with their muskets at the ready ran back across the bog as quickly as they could.

'Look, it's the water-spaniel,' said Joshua. 'It's found something.'

Beyond the running soldiers, they could just make out the dark brown shape of the dog, its tail wagging excitedly among the withered grass at the edge of a bog-hole. For a moment, they half expected to see a snipe rising into the cool evening air, but then realized there would be no birds there now, not after the first search. A few moments later, they saw a muddy figure dragging himself out of the bog-hole. He had a blunderbuss in his hands, and it was clean and shiny, as if he had been holding it above the water, but when he pointed it at the soldiers nothing happened. Immediately the soldiers closed in on him and several jabbed at him with their bayonets. Slowly he dropped to one knee and it was clear to all who watched from the edge of the bog that Archer the outlaw had at long last been captured.

Knowing that they had a dangerous prisoner on their hands, the cavalrymen moved the onlookers back. Joshua and Sammy sprinted ahead and waited near Jemmy O'Brien's cabin to see what was going to happen next. A short time later, Archer was marched into the clearing. The light was beginning to fade, but there was no mistaking the short powerful figure they had come to know. He was bleeding here and there from his wounds, and was almost being carried by the yeomen who held him by each arm. But even then they could see that in his own dogged way he was keeping his head erect, his eyes straight ahead of him.

From somewhere close by, the soldiers had procured a horse and cart and, while the horse was yoked up, Captain Dickey and another officer examined Archer's blunderbuss and pistols with great interest. Archer himself was now lying on the ground, his head propped up against the roots of a tree. He was closely guarded by several soldiers, and when the cart was ready he was hauled to his feet. Whether it was because he was wounded, or considered too dangerous, Joshua and Sammy couldn't tell, but he was now lifted on to the cart and tied down by his hands and feet. In this undignified manner, he was carted off to Ballymena, surrounded by a large number of soldiers and followed by a growing number of people, as word spread, that the outlaw had been captured.

It seemed odd to Joshua and Sammy that throughout the whole episode Jemmy O'Brien was nowhere to be seen. At first they thought that perhaps he had made himself scarce, in case he might be accused of being an accomplice, Archer having been captured so near his cabin. But then they wondered – as indeed others were to wonder for many a long day – if there was another reason. For it had now become obvious that the soldiers who had gone to the Star Bog had been acting on good information.

17

Keeping Secrets

The bell of the clock on the Moravian church rang out across the River Main. Spring was in the air but there was still a chill in the wind. Crossing the stepping–stones quickly so as not to overbalance and end up in the river, Joshua waited for his friend to follow, then both made their way over to the settlement. Fresh supplies had come in from the East India Company and Joshua was taking a small gift of tea to Sister Hannah. He was also looking forward to having a chat with Brother Fridlezius who, he heard, had been in to see Thomas Archer.

Having delivered the tea to Sister Hannah and, as usual, received a gift of herbal mixture in return, they made their way over to the church. Checking the house at one end, then the other, they found Brother Fridlezius seated at the long table, updating the settlement's diary under the watchful eye of the portrait of its founder, John Cennick.

'Is it true you were in to see Thomas Archer?' asked Joshua.

Brother Fridlezius smiled and nodded. But even though Archer had on more than one occasion struck fear into the settlement, it was a smile which somehow also conveyed a feeling of regret that he should have found a fellow human being in such a predicament. Leafing back a page or two he pressed the diary flat so that they could read what had been entered.

'Brother Fridlezius,' recorded the spindly writing, 'went to Ballymena where he recognized Archer, the ringleader of a band of banditti who had committed so many outrages in our district... Archer was apprehended by a party of soldiers and dangerously wounded in the act of being taken. Bro. Fridlezius was present at the Court Martial that was held in the place where the prisoner was confined to his bed on account of his wounds and was convicted of having murdered a man whose two sisters gave evidences against him.'

'Mr Love,' said Joshua.

'Did he say why he killed him?' asked Sammy.

Brother Fridlezius turned around, and somehow his pale gaunt face and his black clothes seemed to match the mood of the occasion. 'He said very little.'

'Uncle Matthew – he lives out in Kildowney – says the word out there is that Mr Love recognized Archer at Kilrea fair.'

'There was bad blood between them before that,' explained Sammy.

'And Mr Love told him he would tell the redcoats where he was,' added Joshua.

'Could well be,' said Brother Fridlezius. 'They said there had been some altercation on the public road all right.'

'Is he badly wounded?' asked Joshua.

Brother Fridlezius nodded. 'Not that it makes much difference now.'

'Do you think it's true,' asked Sammy, 'that Jemmy O'Brien betrayed him?'

Brother Fridlezius shrugged. 'Who knows?'

'They say Archer was asleep in his cabin when it happened,' said Joshua.

'And that O'Brien poured water into his pistols and put a small nail into the touchhole of his blunderbuss,' said Sammy.

'Then sent word to the military and went to a neighbour's place to await their arrival,' said Joshua.

'But that his son, who didn't know about the plot, saw the soldiers and roused Archer,' Sammy continued. 'They say Archer picked up his blunderbuss and ran for his life, and that the soldiers opened fire and wounded him before he hid in the bog-hole.'

'That's what the first report in the paper suggested,'

Updating the settlement's diary

said Brother Fridlezius. 'That the man of the house – it didn't mention O'Brien by name, mind you – had poured water into Archer's firearms. But now Captain Dickey has put up notices saying that isn't true.'

Joshua nodded. 'We've seen them. He also says O'Brien isn't the person who gave the information.'

'But then he would say that, wouldn't he?' said Sammy.

Brother Fridlezius took up his quill again and turned to the page where he had been writing. 'Well, as I said, it doesn't really matter now, does it?'

Monday came and Joshua didn't go to school. Nor was Sammy at his loom. Like the rest of the town's population, they crossed the river and climbed the hill to the Norman mound known as the Moat. It was March 10th, 1800, almost two years since the army of the United Irishmen had marched into the town and laid siege to the Market House. Now the assembled townspeople were about to witness an event that would finally bring the rebellion in their area to a close.

In the middle of a strong force of soldiers, Thomas Archer, the last of the United leaders, stood on a flat cart, his hands tied behind his back. The cart had been drawn up under the tall ash tree that grew beside the mound. A rope had been thrown over the branch that stretched out across the track and Joshua couldn't help thinking of the day Sammy and he had sat on the very same branch, looking at the yeomen who had ridden underneath. That was just after their encounter with Archer and his men on the way to Gracehill. How much had happened since, he thought, and how much things had changed.

Wounded though he was, Archer still looked defiant and, with the noose now around his neck, he began to speak. 'If all had kept their secrets in their breasts as I have done,' he began. Immediately there were shouts of 'Silence' and 'Drive on the cart.' The cart moved forward and he swung free, struggling for air.

Finding a curious mixture of emotions coursing through

his mind, Joshua stared at the ground and dug his hands deep into the pockets of his breeches. As he did so, his fingers felt the cavalry button that had fallen from Master Davison's pocket. Taking it out, he looked at the letters on it and thought of the day the master had been killed. He also thought of Mr Love and how he had been killed.

'Come on, Sammy,' he said. 'Let's go.'

Sammy nodded, and together they walked back down the hill.

After a short time, Archer's body was put in irons and hung on a high gallows on top of the Moat, as a warning to others not to follow his example. Eventually some young men took down his remains, smuggled them across the river and buried them in the churchyard where Master Davison had been buried two years before.

Having hidden out in the mountains beyond the Bann, Captain Nevin sailed from Magilligan in County Derry and settled in America. He wrote long letters to his family, expressing his intention to come home for a visit, but never did. He died at Knoxville, Tennessee, in 1806.

Colonel Clavering died in obscurity in Scotland.

The Irish Parliament voted itself out of existence, and on January 1st, 1801, the Act of Union came into effect.

To this day, the two carvings done by Brother Fridlezius can be seen above the doors of the Moravian Church at Gracehill. And the people of Ballymena still talk of Thomas Archer who was hanged on the Moat.

Historical Footnote

While this book is based on fact, it is a work of fiction and I have taken a certain amount of poetic licence. For example, as Thomas Archer, Roddy McCorley and Dr Linn came from the same general area of County Antrim, I have assumed that they would have known and consorted with one another. Although John Nevin was not from Ballymena, he did take part in the rebellion in the town and, as a captain in the United Irishmen, would surely have known Archer too. Immediately after the rebellion, Nevin went into hiding near Cloughmills. It was not far from there that Archer is believed to have had his hide-out, and I don't think it is stretching the imagination to bring them together.

The smuggling of Captain Nevin over the River Bann in a barrel is recounted in *Memories of '98* by W. S. Smith, published in Belfast in 1895, although the episode appears to have occurred much earlier than my story suggests. At that particular time it was customary to make jugs commemorating certain events, for example, the fall of the Bastille during the French Revolution. Others commemorated more local events. In Ballymoney, where Nevin came from and where he apparently got his military training in the local Volunteers, jugs were made with inscriptions declaring success to the Volunteer societies, free trade in Ireland, and peace and independence.

Not surprisingly, the account of Nevin's escape given by W. S. Smith also relates that relatives and friends of the young exile had a number of jugs made after his death in America. These bore the inscription, 'To the memory of John Nevin of Kilmoyle, who was by the Foes of Reform banished from his native home in June 1798. He lived in the state of exile for seven years, eleven months, eight days, and departed this life in Knoxville, Tennessee, 19th May, 1806. Much lamented by all his friends, acquaintances and friends to their country.' Like the Volunteer jugs, some of those commemorating Nevin also bore the motto, 'Peace and Independence.'

The discovery of Archer in the Star bog by the water-spaniel that accompanied the military is recounted by W.S. Smith. It is also recorded in a detailed account of the rebellion published in the *Ballymena Observer* in 1857 and reprinted in a booklet called *Old Ballymena* which is available in the town. For the purposes of my story, I have suggested that the spaniel belonged to Captain Dickey, although there is no historical reference to support that. As for Archer's last words, they are quoted in both pub-lications.

The suggestion that Master Davison fired cavalry buttons, nails and other materials during the battle of the Market House, in an effort to conserve his ammunition, is made in the *Observer* account. However, in a letter to the newspaper, a correspondent pointed out that cavalry buttons that were unearthed in the old churchyard – and which gave rise to the story – could have come from the clothing of the member of the Dunseverick Cavalry who was killed in a fall from the Market House.

The moiley 'monster' mentioned in this story may be traced to two sources: *The Year of Liberty*, by Thomas Pakenham, recounts that when people who had betrayed the United Irishmen disappeared, people would say, 'Moiley has eaten them.' Similarly *Old Ballymena* says that, in the language of the day, such people were con-signed to a 'voracious though fabulous cow' called Moiley, who never failed to eat them. Here, I might add, that when I was growing up in Ballymena, a cow without horns was always known as a moiley.

Old Ballymena records that Archer and Mr Love 'had previously been engaged in a violent altercation upon the public road', and some years ago a neighbour of mine in Ballymena, Mr William Rodgers of Laymore, shed new light on this. Mr Rodgers, who was in his eighties at the time, said his grandfather told him he knew Archer. He also told him how a local farmer had recognized the outlaw at Kilrea fair. The farmer threatened to 'tell the redcoats' and that night Archer arrived at the man's home and killed him.

While the name of the farmer differs in the two accounts, they seem to relate to the same incident, and the account given by Mr Rodgers, which he confirmed to me shortly before he died, would seem to indicate the real motive for the murder.

During my research, I was fortunate to locate a descendant of Mr Love, Ernest Love of Kilcreen. He told me that Archer's victim was his great-grandfather's brother. He also directed me to the house on Kildowney Hill, where the shooting took place. It is now occupied by Gordon Stewart and his wife Aileen. They told me that after the shooting Mr Love managed to drag himself upstairs to a bedroom, where he died. According to tradition, the bloodstains were visible on the stairs for many years afterwards.

A study of evidence relating to Roddy McCorley was compiled by Anne Fay of Magherafelt when she was head of history at St Mary's College, Portglenone. In it she relates that, about fifty years after he was hanged on the bridge at Toome, his remains were found by his nephew during work on a new bridge and reinterred in Duneane Churchyard.

The magistrate who was attacked by the United Irishmen was the Rev William McCleverty. According to J.B. Leslie in *Clergy of Connor* (1993), he died in 1799 from wounds received in the rebellion.

The annoyance of the townspeople at the billeting of troops in the houses and churches in Ballymena is recorded in the *Observer's* account of the rebellion. However, it would appear to have occurred somewhat later than I have suggested. The newspaper's account says Colonel Clavering and his men retired from the area within the following month and the churches were taken over as winter quarters for some of the troops who succeeded them.

Acknowledgements

I am very grateful to the Rev Richard Ingham for allowing me to examine some of the entries in the diaries at Gracehill, relating to events at the Moravian settlement and surrounding areas in 1798. Subsequently, I was glad to hear from his successor, the Rev Victor Launder, that the work of putting the diaries on microfilm had been completed.

A History of Gracehill, which was brought up to date by Brother Ingham, was also of great help, and I wish to thank Dr Eull Dunlop, secretary of the Mid-Antrim Historical Group, who brought this booklet and many other valuable references to my attention.

My thanks also to Mrs Rosalie White, a member of the Moravian community in Gracehill, for her advice; F. Glenn Thompson in Dublin, and Tom Wylie, curator of the local history department of the Ulster Museum in Belfast, for information about military units, uniforms, weapons and flags of the period; the staffs of the Linenhall Library in Belfast, and the Ulster Folk and Transport Museum in Holywood, County Down; Lynn Buick, Pat Lane and other members of the staff at the area reference library in Ballymena; Leni McCullagh in the reference and illustrations library in RTE; Sam Clarke, Bill Dallas, Derek and Gertie Goodhue, and the many others who provided me with historical references, information and advice. I am also grateful to Brendan Slein of Securicor, who was so helpful in getting material to Ballymena and London at short notice.

TOM McCAUGHREN

For his twelfth book, Tom McCaughren delves into the dramatic events that took place in his home town, Ballymena in Country Antrim, in 1798.

He has also written five adventure books for The Children's Press, and a highly acclaimed thriller for teenagers, *Rainbows of the Moon* (Anvil Books). Set on the Irish border during the present 'troubles', it was short-listed for the Irish Book Awards in 1990 and has now been translated into several languages. His four 'fox' books (Wolfhound Press) have also been widely translated, and his books are now read in French, Flemish/Dutch, Swedish, German, Japanese and Latvian.

His awards include the Reading Association of Ireland Book Award (1985), the Irish Book Awards Medal (1987), the White Ravens selection of the International Youth Library in Munich (1988), the Bisto Book of the Decade Award (1980–1990), and the Oscar Wilde Society's Literary Recognition Award (1992).

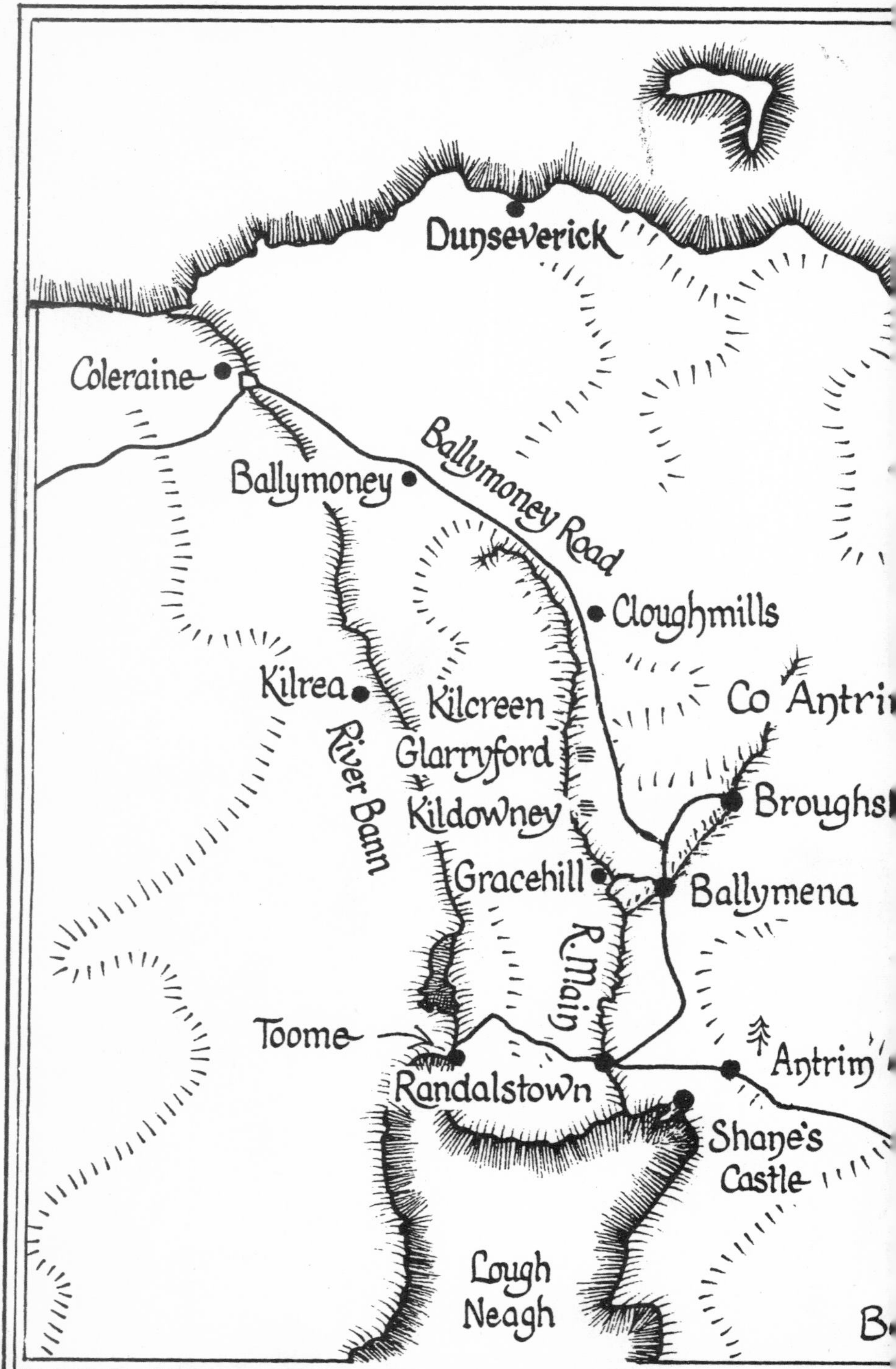
Dunseverick
Coleraine
Ballymoney
Ballymoney Road
Cloughmills
Kilrea
Kilcreen
River Bann
Glarryford
Kildowney
Gracehill
Co Antri
Broughs
Ballymena
R. Main
Toome
Randalstown
Antrim
Shane's Castle
Lough Neagh
B